TORTURE

TORTURE

When the Unthinkable Is Morally Permissible

moral 23 80

convers. 81

moral IX

Mirko Bagaric

Julie Clarke

STATE UNIVERSITY OF NEW YORK PRESS

Published by
State University of New York Press, Albany

© 2007 State University of New York

For information, contact
State University of New York Press, Albany, NY
www.sunypress.edu

Production by Marilyn P. Semerad
Marketing by Fran Keneston

Library of Congress Cataloging in Publication Data

Bagaric, Mirko.
  Torture : when the unthinkable is morally permissible / Mirko
Bagaric, Julie Clarke.
    p. cm.
  Includes bibliographical references and index.
  ISBN-13: 978-0-7914-7153-1 (hardcover : alk. paper)
  ISBN-13: 978-0-7914-7154-8 (pbk.: alk. paper) 1. Torture—Moral
and ethical aspects. 2. Torture—United States. 3. Political prisoners—
Abuse of—United States. 4. Human rights. I. Clarke, Julie, 1952–
II. Title.

HV8593B35 2007
364.6'7—dc22
                                                    2006027537

10 9 8 7 6 5 4 3 2 1

1/09

Contents

Preface

The following opinion piece, which one of us had published in *The Age* (Melbourne) and *Sydney Morning Herald* on May 17, 2005 caused worldwide outrage.

THE CASE FOR TORTURE

"Our reflex rejection of torture needs to be replaced by recognition that it can be a moral means of saving lives."

Recent events stemming from the "war on terrorism" have highlighted the prevalence of torture. This is despite the fact that torture is almost universally deplored. The formal prohibition against torture is absolute—there are no exceptions to it.

The belief that torture is always wrong is, however, misguided and symptomatic of the alarmist and reflexive responses typically emanating from social commentators. It is this type of absolutist and short-sighted rhetoric that lies at the core of many distorted moral judgments that we as a community continue to make, resulting in an enormous amount of injustice and suffering in our society and far beyond our borders.

Torture is permissible where the evidence suggests that this is the only means, due to the immediacy of the situation, to save the life of an innocent person. The reason that torture in such a case is defensible and necessary is because the justification manifests from the closest thing we have to an inviolable right: the right to self-defense, which of course extends to the defense of another. Given the choice between inflicting a relatively small level of harm on a wrongdoer and saving an innocent person, it is verging on moral indecency to prefer the interests of the wrongdoer.

The analogy with self-defense is sharpened by considering the hostage-taking scenario, where a wrongdoer takes a hostage and points a gun to the hostage's head, threatening to kill the hostage unless a certain (unreasonable) demand is met. In such a case it is not only permissible but desirable for police to shoot (and kill) the wrongdoer if they get a "clear shot." This is especially true if it's known that the wrongdoer has a history of serious violence, and hence is more likely to carry out the threat.

It is indefensible to suggest that there should be an absolute ban on torture. There is no logical or moral difference between this scenario and one where there is overwhelming evidence that a wrongdoer has kidnapped an innocent person and informs police that the victim will be killed by a co-offender if certain demands are not met.

In the hostage scenario, it is universally accepted that it is permissible to violate the right to life of the aggressor to save an innocent person. How can it be wrong to violate an even less important right (the right to physical integrity) by torturing the aggressor in order to save a life in the second scenario?

There are three main counterarguments to even the above limited approval of torture. The first is the slippery slope argument: if you start allowing torture in a limited context, the situations in which it will be used will increase.

This argument is not sound in the context of torture. First, the floodgates are already open—torture is used widely, despite the absolute legal prohibition against it. Amnesty International has recently reported that it had received, during 2003, reports of torture and ill-treatment from 132 countries, including the United States, Japan, and France. It is, in fact, arguable that it is the existence of an unrealistic absolute ban that has driven torture beneath the radar of accountability, and that legalization in very rare circumstances would in fact reduce instances of it.

The second main argument is that torture will dehumanize society. This is no more true in relation to torture than it is with self-defense, and in fact the contrary is true. A society that elects to favor the interests of wrongdoers over those of the innocent, when a choice must be made between the two, is in need of serious ethical rewiring.

A third counterargument is that we can never be totally sure that torturing a person will in fact result in us saving an innocent life. This, however, is the same situation as in all cases of self-defense. To revisit the hostage example, the hostage-taker's gun might in fact be empty, yet it is still permissible to shoot. As with any decision, we must decide on the best evidence at the time.

Torture in order to save an innocent person is the only situation where it is clearly justifiable. This means that the recent high-profile incidents of torture, apparently undertaken as punitive measures or in a bid to acquire information where there was no evidence of an immediate risk to the life of an innocent person, were reprehensible.

Will a real-life situation actually occur where the only option is between torturing a wrongdoer and saving an innocent person? Perhaps not. However, a minor alteration to the Douglas Wood situation illustrates that the issue is far from moot. If Western forces in Iraq arrested one of Mr. Wood's captors, it would be a perverse ethic that required us to respect the physical integrity of the captor, and not torture him to ascertain Mr. Wood's whereabouts, in preference to taking all possible steps to save Mr. Wood.

Even if a real-life situation where torture is justifiable does not eventuate, the above argument in favor of torture in limited circumstances needs to be made because it will encourage the community to think more carefully about moral judgments we collectively hold that are the cause of an enormous amount of suffering in the world.

First, no right or interest is absolute. Secondly, rights must always yield to consequences, which are the ultimate criteria upon which the soundness of a decision is gauged. Lost lives hurt a lot more than bent principles.

Thirdly, we must take responsibility not only for the things that we do, but also for the things that we can—but fail to—prevent. The retort that we are not responsible for the lives lost through a decision not to torture a wrongdoer because we did not create the situation is code for moral indifference.

Equally vacuous is the claim that we in the affluent West have no responsibility for more than 13,000 people dying daily due to starvation. Hopefully, the debate on torture will prompt us to correct some of these fundamental failings.

Responses (mainly criticisms) to the piece flooded in not only from academics but from large numbers of lay people and politicians past and present, including former Australian Prime Minister Malcolm Fraser.

Yet barely six months later (following terrorist bombings in the United Kingdom, Jordan, and Bali and the arrest of terrorists suspects in Australia) the United States admitted that it engages in the practice of "rendition" (which involves abducting suspects and sending them to other parts of the world where they are subjected to coercive interrogation); the United Kingdom introduced "shoot to kill laws"; the U.S. President George Bush attempted (unsuccessfully as it transpired) to persuade Congress to reject a bill that would expressly prohibit "cruel, inhuman or degrading treatment or punishment of anyone in U.S. custody" and a clear majority of Americans believe that torture in the circumstances we outline is acceptable.

This book examines the moral status of torture. The issue captivates academics, social commentators, lawyers, and lay people alike because while the act is ostensibly brutal, it has the potential to achieve compassionate outcomes in the form of saving the lives of innocent people. Torture causes our emotion to conflict with our reason. This book explains and resolves this conflict.

The book goes beyond the narrow practice of torture. It analyzes the implications that the formal prohibition against torture has for moral theory. It is argued that the absolute ban on torture reveals a fundamental shortcoming of our moral code—in fact there are no absolutes in properly informed normative thinking.

When rights clash and we have a choice between preserving a wrongdoer's right not to be physically harmed and the right to life of innocent people, it is absurd to suggest that we should protect the wrongdoer. A preference for the interests of the wrongdoer can occur only in a moral vacuum, devoid of an overarching moral theory.

Chapter 1 provides an overview of the practice of torture and themes discussed in the book. Chapter 2 discusses the current legal position and the reality of torture. The paradox of torture emerges readily when, despite its absolute prohibition, we see that it is practiced in more than one hundred countries. The moral status of torture is considered in chapter 3.

After concluding that torture is permissible where it is the only means available to save innocent life, in chapters 4, 5, 6, and 7 we consider the main counterarguments to our proposal. They are the slippery slope argument, the argument that torture is not effective as an information-gathering device, that it is inhumane and antidemocratic.

In chapter 8, we explain why the debate is so divisive. Chapter 9 examines the wider implications that the torture debate has for our moral code.

Acknowledgments

We wish to thank the *University of San Francisco Law Review* for allowing us to reproduce earlier portions of the following papers in this book:

- Not Enough (Official) Torture in the World? The Circumstances in Which Torture Is Morally Justifiable 39 *University of San Francisco Law Review* 581 (2005).

- Tortured Responses (A Reply to the Critics): Physically Persuading Suspects Is Morally Preferable to Allowing the Innocent to Be Murdered 40 *University of San Francisco Law Review* 1 (2006).

CHAPTER ONE

Introduction

Overview of the Torture Debate

OVERVIEW OF WHEN TORTURE IS PERMISSIBLE

Recent events stemming from the "war on terrorism" have high-lighted the prevalence of torture. Torture is almost universally deplored. It is prohibited by international law and is not officially sanctioned by the domestic laws of any state.[1] The formal prohibition against torture is absolute—there are no exceptions to it. This is not only pragmatically unrealistic, but unsound at a normative level. Despite the absolute ban on torture, it is widely used. Contrary to common belief, torture is not the preserve of despot military regimes in third-world nations. For example, there are serious concerns regarding the treatment by the United States of senior Al Qaeda leader Khalid Shaikh Mohammad.[2] There is also irrefutable evidence that the United States tortured large numbers of Iraqi prisoners, as well as strong evidence that it tortured prisoners at Guantánamo Bay prison in Cuba, where suspected Al Qaeda terrorists are held.[3] More generally, Alan Dershowitz has noted, "[C]ountries all over the world violate the Geneva Accords [prohibiting torture]. They do it secretly and hypocritically, the way the French did it in Algeria."[4]

1

Dershowitz has also argued that torture should be made lawful. His argument is based on a harm minimization rationale from the perspective of victims of torture. He has said, "Of course it would be best if we didn't use torture at all, but if the United States is going to continue to torture people, we need to make the process legal and accountable."[5] Our argument goes one step beyond this. We argue that torture is indeed morally defensible, not just pragmatically desirable. The harm minimization rationale is used to supplement our argument.

The pejorative connotation associated with torture should be abolished. A dispassionate analysis of the propriety of torture indicates that it is morally justifiable in limited circumstances. At the outset of this discussion, it is useful to encourage readers to seriously contemplate moving from the question of whether torture is *ever* defensible to the issue of the circumstances in which it is morally permissible.

Consider the following example: A terrorist network has activated a large bomb on one of hundreds of commercial planes carrying more than three hundred passengers that are flying somewhere in the world at any point in time. The bomb is set to explode in thirty minutes. The leader of the terrorist organization announces this via a statement on the Internet. He states that the bomb was planted by one of his colleagues at one of the major airports in the world in the past few hours. No details are provided regarding the location of the plane where the bomb is located. Unbeknownst to him, he was under police surveillance and is immediately apprehended by police. The terrorist leader refuses to answer any police questions, declaring that the passengers must die and will shortly.

Consider further the following example: Aljazeera has broadcast a video that shows notorious terrorist Osama bin Laden and four masked men with machine guns holding captive twelve U.S. civilians that were working in Iraq. The hostages were recently kidnapped by his terrorist network. Bin Laden states that if the United States does not withdraw all of its soldiers from Iraq within one week, he will torture to death each hostage. One hostage will be tortured to death each day if the deadline is not met. The United States refuses to accede to his request. A frantic and wide-ranging search to find the hostages is unsuccessful. Nine days after the video is released, the mutilated and decapitated bodies (showing obvious signs of torture prior to being killed) of two of the hostages are found. Bin Laden is also found several hours later, near the border of Iraq and Syria. He is questioned regarding the location of the ten remaining hostages. Defiantly, he states that he has left orders to continue with the torture and murder of one prisoner per day. He refuses to answer any more questions, other than to assert that the location of the hostages is very secure and the United States will never find it. What possible justification can there be for not torturing bin Laden in order to try to prevent the torture and decapitation of more innocent hostages?

Who would deny that all possible means should be used to extract the details of the plane and the location of the bomb in the first example and the location of the hostages in the second? The answer is not many.[6] The passengers and hostages, their relatives and friends, and many in society would expect that all means should be used to extract the information.

Although the above examples are hypothetical, the force of examples cannot be dismissed on that basis. As C. L. Ten notes, "fantastic examples" that raise fundamental issues for consideration, such as whether it is proper to torture wrongdoers, play an important role in the evaluation of moral principles and theories.[7] These examples sharpen contrasts and illuminate the logical conclusions of the respective principles to test the true strength of our commitment to the principles. Thus, fantastic examples cannot be dismissed summarily merely because they are "simply" hypothetical.

Real life is, of course, rarely this clear cut, but there are certainly scenarios approaching this degree of desperation, which raise for discussion whether it is justifiable to inflict harm on one person to reduce a greater level of harm occurring to a large number of blameless people. Ultimately, torture is simply a very acute example of where the interests of one agent are sacrificed for the greater good. As a community, we are willing to accept this principle. Torture is no different in nature to conduct that we sanction in other circumstances. It should be viewed in this light. Given this, it is illogical to insist on a blanket prohibition against torture.

It is contended that torture is morally permissible where it is the only means available to save innocent lives. Torture should only be used where the threat is imminent, there are no other means of alleviating the threat, and the suspect is known to have the relevant information. Torture is justifiable in these circumstances because it is less bad to inflict physical harm on a person than to allow large numbers (or in some cases a single person) to die. When rights clash and only one right can be protected we should opt for the higher-order right. To this end, the right to life is more important than the right to physical integrity.

We condone torture only in life-saving circumstances. As is discussed in chapter 6, torture has been effectively used on many occasions to thwart attacks against civilians, but it is not clear that there were not other means available to prevent these attacks. Thus, our proposal would legitimize very few reported instances of torture that have occurred.

More elaborately, the factors that are relevant to determining whether torture is permissible and the degree of torture that is appropriate are: (1) the number of lives at risk; (2) the immediacy of the harm; (3) the availability of other means to acquire the information; (4) the level of wrongdoing of the agent; and (5) the likelihood that the agent actually does possess the relevant information.

The moral arguments in favor of torture are discussed in chapter 3. It is argued that torture is no different from other forms of morally permissible behavior and is justifiable on a utilitarian ethic. It is also argued that, on close reflection, torture is also justifiable against a backdrop of a nonconsequentialist rights-based ethic, which is widely regarded as prohibiting torture in all circumstances. Thus, we conclude that torture is morally justifiable in rare circumstances, irrespective of which normative theory one adopts.

Prior to addressing these issues, in the next chapter we analyze the meaning of torture and the nature and scope of the legal prohibition against torture.

OVERVIEW OF ARGUMENTS AGAINST TORTURE

In chapters 4, 5, 6, and 7, we consider the main counter arguments to our proposal.

The first is the slippery slope or thin edge of wedge argument. If torture is condoned in the circumstances we set out it will, so the argument runs, result in the widespread use of torture. Secondly, and related to this point, is that legalizing torture will dehumanize society.

A more pragmatic objection to our proposal is that torture does not work. Suspects that are tortured will, supposedly, not "fess up." This is the third main line of criticism. The fourth point made by some critics is that legalization of torture would be "antidemocratic."

Our responses are relatively short. The task has been attenuated by the fact that the critics have not attempted to undermine the underlying (consequentialist) ethic upon which our proposal is based. Rather, they have been aghast at the conclusions to which utilitarianism commits us (condoning torture), and some critics have doubted whether a proper consideration of all the relevant variables leads us to condoning torture in any circumstances. There has been no attempt by the critics to develop an alternative normative theory that justifies their stance on torture and can be invoked to provide answers across a range of moral issues.

There is one qualification to the statement that the critics have not sought to undermine the moral ethic we endorse. Many critics have stated that our proposal is flawed because "the end does not justify the means." This is more akin to a "throwaway line," than a considered and measured criticism. Nevertheless, despite how one chooses to characterize the criticism, it has been said frequently enough to merit a response. This is dealt with in chapter 10.

THE WIDER IMPLICATIONS OF THE TORTURE DEBATE TO MORAL THEORY

There are two other central matters that are addressed in this book. The first, discussed in chapter 8, is what we consider to be the most powerful objection to our proposal. That is the argument that rights do not clash in the situations where we believe life-saving torture is permissible, because, if innocent people are killed by others, we bear no responsibility for this since the killings are not committed by us. This argument is flawed but it gets to the heart of the issue and offers the best explanation as to why the torture debate has been so divisive.

An explanation is fitting because it is rare for a proposed legal reform to generate so much (ill) feeling. The critics of our proposal are well intentioned and their responses are driven by a revulsion toward the prospect of torturing a person. We too find this abhorrent (but less so than allowing innocent people to be murdered). If we are all so appalled by the prospect of deliberately inflicting pain and accept that it is an important moral maxim, how can it be that such vastly different conclusions are reached regarding the moral status of torture? In chapter 8, we get to the heart of this dilemma.

In chapter 9, we discuss why torture matters, far beyond the contours of the discussion at hand. The circumstances in which life-saving torture are justifiable will occur infrequently. Nevertheless, the debate is important because it has implications well beyond the narrow practice of torture. The supposed absolute ban on torture highlights much about what is wrong with contemporary moral thinking. The critics are committed to the nonsensical conclusion that the right to physical integrity (of the suspect) is more important than the right to life (of the potential victims) and seem resolute in their conviction not to extend their sphere of moral concern beyond the interests of the suspect to other affected parties, namely the victims. An analysis of this type can only occur in the context of a moral fog, which is where contemporary moral thought finds itself.

It is in the context of such an environment that moral issues are often resolved not on the basis of clear thinking and reasoned analysis but according to who makes the loudest emotive retort. To this end, we undertake a "meta-analysis" of the debate at hand and the way it has been played out. The emotion that this debate has generated underscores the view that moral debates, at least in part, often turn into emotion-venting episodes.

This can result in even the best-intentioned participant engaging in "reverse extremism." (It is reverse because it is based on a feeling of righteousness.) Extremism in all its manifestations, at least potentially, stifles debate and ultimately leads to stereotypical views of people. Indeed many of the torture opponents have engaged in the exact type of besmirching that leads to polarized communities and violence by some groups toward others.

The reason for this and how to avoid it in the future is examined in chapter 9.

CHAPTER TWO

Torture

Reality and Legal Position

THE LAW ON TORTURE

Pursuant to international law, "torture" is defined as:

> Any act by which severe pain or suffering, whether physical or mental, is intentionally inflicted on a person for such purposes as obtaining from him or a third person information or a confession, punishing him for an act he or a third person has committed or is suspected of having committed, or intimidating or coercing him or a third person, or for any reason based on discrimination of any kind, when such pain or suffering is inflicted by or at the instigation of or with the consent or acquiescence of a public official or other person acting in an official capacity. It does not include pain or suffering arising only from, inherent in, or incidental to lawful sanctions.[1]

Torture is prohibited by a number of international documents.[2] It is also considered to carry a special status in customary international law, that of *jus cogens*, which is a "peremptory norm" of customary international law.[3] The significance of this is that customary international law is binding on all states, even if they have not ratified a particular treaty. At treaty level, there are both general treaties that proscribe torture and specific treaties banning the practice.

In terms of general treaties, torture is prohibited by a number of international and regional treaties. These include Article 5 of the Universal Declaration of Human Rights (1948)[4]; Articles 7 and 10(1) of the International Covenant on Civil and Political Rights (1966)[5]; Article 3 of the European Convention on Human Rights (1950)[6]; Article 5(2) of the American Convention on Human Rights (1978)[7]; and Article 5 of the African Charter on Human and People's Rights (1981).[8]

In addition to these instruments, which set out a range of human rights, the international community has implemented specific treaties addressing torture. The main treaties are the United Nations Convention against Torture, 1984; the European Convention for the Prevention of Torture and Inhuman and Degrading Treatment or Punishment, 1987[9]; and the Inter-American Convention to Prevent and Punish Torture, 1985.[10]

The rigidity of the rule against torture is exemplified by the fact that it has a nonderogable status in human rights law. That is, there are no circumstances in which torture is permissible. This prohibition is made clear in Article 2(2) of the UN Convention against Torture, which states, "No exceptional circumstances whatsoever, whether a state of war or a threat of war, internal political instability or any other public emergency, may be invoked as a justification of torture."[11]

Thus, the right not to be tortured is absolute.

> There are no circumstances in which states can set aside or restrict this obligation, even in times of war or other emergency threatening the life of the nation, which may justify the suspension or limitation of some other rights. States are also restricted from making derogations which may put individuals at risk of torture or ill-treatment—for example, by allowing excessive periods of incommunicado detention or denying a

detainee prompt access to a court. This prohibition operates irrespective of circumstances or attributes, such as the status of the victim or, if he or she is a criminal suspect, upon the crimes that the victim is suspected of having committed.

State officials are prohibited from inflicting, instigating or tolerating the torture or other cruel, inhuman or degrading treatment or punishment of any person. An order from a superior officer or a public authority may not be invoked as a justification for torture. States are also required to ensure that all acts of torture are offences under their criminal law, establish criminal jurisdiction over such acts, investigate all such acts and hold those responsible for committing them to account.[12]

This absolute prohibition is frequently highlighted by Amnesty International and other human rights organizations. For example, Amnesty International states, "The law is unequivocal—torture is absolutely prohibited in all circumstances. . . . The right to be free from torture is absolute. It cannot be denied to anyone in any circumstances."[13]

Torture is also prohibited as a war crime, pursuant to humanitarian law.[14] In addition, torture is considered to be a crime against humanity when the acts are perpetrated as part of a widespread or systematic attack against a civilian population, whether or not they are committed in the course of an armed conflict.[15]

As with many legal precepts, the black letter law must be considered against the context of reality. As we shall see in the section below titled Widespread Use of Torture, various forms of torture are used despite its legal prohibition.

FORMS OF TORTURE

As is noted by Dershowitz, torture comes in many different forms and intensities:

Torture is a continuum and the two extremes are on the one hand torturing someone to death—that is, torturing an enemy to death so that others will know that if you are caught, you will be caused excruciating pain—that's torture as a deterrent. . . . At the other extreme, there's nonlethal torture which leaves only psychological scars. The perfect example of this is a sterilized needle inserted under the fingernail, causing unbearable pain but no possible long-term damage. These are very different phenomena. What they have in common of course is that they allow the government physically to come into contact with you in order to produce pain.[16]

Various methods of torture have and continue to be applied in a multitude of countries. The most common methods are beating, electric shock, rape and sexual abuse, mock execution or threat of death, and prolonged solitary confinement.[17] Other common methods include sleep and sensory deprivation, suspension of the body,[18] "shackling interrogees in contorted painful positions" or in "painful stretching positions,"[19] and applying pressure to sensitive areas, such as the "neck, throat, genitals, chest, and head."[20]

THE BENEFITS OF TORTURE: AN EFFECTIVE INFORMATION-GATHERING DEVICE

The main benefit of torture is that it is an effective means of gathering information. Humans have an intense desire to avoid pain, no matter how short-term, and most will comply with the demands of a torturer to avoid the pain. Often the threat of torture alone will evoke cooperation. To this end, Dershowitz cites a kidnapping case in Germany in which the son of a distinguished banker was kidnapped.[21] The eleven-year-old boy had been missing for three days. The police had in their custody a man they were convinced had perpetrated the kidnapping. The man was taken into custody after being seen collecting a ransom that was paid by the boy's family.[22] During seven hours of interrogation the man "toyed" with police, leading them to one false location after another.[23] After exhausting all lawful means of interrogation, the deputy commissioner of the Frankfurt police instructed his officers, in writing, that they could try to extract information "by means of the infliction of pain, under medical supervision and subject to prior warning."[24] Ten minutes after the warning was given the suspect told the police where the boy was; unfortunately, the boy was already dead, having been killed shortly after the kidnapping.[25] It is easy to multiply examples of torture being an effective information-gathering technique.

As we shall see in chapter 6, one of the main criticisms of the proposal to sanction life-saving torture is that torture is not an effective information-gathering device. As part of the counter to this criticism, numerous other incidents of effective torture are discussed in chapter 6.

THE WIDESPREAD USE OF TORTURE

Torture around the World

Despite the contemporary abhorrence against it, dozens of countries continue to use torture. A study of 195 countries and territories by Amnesty International between 1997 and mid-2000 found reports of torture or ill-treatment by state officials in more than 150 countries,[26] and in more than seventy countries that torture or ill-treatment was reported as "widespread or persistent."[27] It is also clear that torture is not limited to military regimes in third-world nations. Amnesty International recently reported that in 2003 it had received reports of torture and ill-treatment from 132 countries, including the United States, Canada, Japan, France, Italy, Spain, and Germany.[28] Israel, for example, officially sanctioned interrogation practices deemed by the UN Committee against Torture to constitute torture[29] until a decision of the Supreme Court of Israel, sitting as the High Court of Justice, in September 1999, ruled a number of these interrogations unlawful absent any clear statutory authorization.[30] Prior to the Israeli Supreme Court ruling, the UN Committee against Torture made the following observations in relation to Israeli interrogation techniques:

> [T]he methods of interrogation, which were described by nongovernmental organizations on the basis of accounts given to them by interrogatees and appear to be applied systematically, were neither confirmed nor denied by Israel. The Committee must therefore assume them to be accurate. Those methods include: (1) restraining in very painful conditions, (2) hooding under special conditions, (3) sounding of loud music for prolonged periods, (4) sleep deprivation for prolonged periods, (5) threats, including death threats, (6) violent shaking, and (7) using cold air to chill, and are, in the Committee's view, breaches of article 16 and also constitute torture as defined in article 1 of the Convention. This conclusion is particularly evident where such methods of interrogation are used in combination, which appears to be the standard case.[31]

Despite the Court's ruling, there is evidence that the practice of torture by the Israeli government continues.[32] This may have been facilitated by the Court's comments that it would accept, in appropriate circumstances, that Israel's General Security Service investigators might "avail themselves of the 'necessity' defense, if criminally indicted," for using the banned interrogation methods.[33] One report cites official statistics between September 1999 and July 2002 that indicate that during that time ninety Palestinians were defined as "ticking bombs" and thus subject to interrogation methods that would constitute torture under international law.[34]

Indeed, a detailed study of forty-eight Palestinian detainees found that interrogees were, in various combinations, frequently beaten, slapped, or kicked, bent and placed in painful positions, violently shaken, deprived of sleep, shackled behind their backs for prolonged periods of cases, cursed at, threatened, degraded and deprived of essential needs, including food, water, and medical care, among other things.[35] In more than 70 percent of cases, three or more of these methods were applied.[36] Extrapolating from this and official data of the number of Palestinian detainees, the study estimated that each month in Israel "ill-treatment reaching the level of torture as defined in international law is inflicted in dozens of cases, and possibly more."[37]

The widespread use of torture is also clearly demonstrated by even a cursory reading of the recent U.S. Department of State Country Information Reports. For example, the report on Turkey provides that torture, beatings, and other abuses by security forces remain widespread.[38]

> Security forces reportedly killed forty-three persons during the year. . . . Security forces continued to use arbitrary arrest and detention, although the number of such incidents declined. . . . The rarity of convictions and the light sentences imposed on police and other security officials for killings and torture continued to foster a climate of impunity. Prosecutions brought by the Government in State Security Courts (SSCs) reflected a legal structure that favored government interests over individual rights. . . . Police beat, abused, detained, and harassed some demonstrators.[39]

The assessment on Pakistan states:

> Security force personnel continued to torture persons in custody throughout the country. For example, according to Human Rights Watch (HRW), Rasheed Azam was beaten and tortured at Khuzdar military cantonment. In September, two prison officials allegedly beat and killed eighteen-year-old Sunil Samuel at Camp Jail in Lahore after he was sexually assaulted by inmates. Over the years, there have been allegations that common torture methods included: beating; burning with cigarettes; whipping the soles of

the feet; sexual assault; prolonged isolation; electric shock; denial of food or sleep; hanging upside down; forced spreading of the legs with bar fetters; and public humiliation.[40]

In relation to China, the report asserts:

The law prohibits torture; however, police and other elements of the security apparatus employed torture and degrading treatment in dealing with some detainees and prisoners. The Prison Law forbids prison guards from extorting confessions by torture, insulting prisoners' dignity, and beating or encouraging others to beat prisoners. While senior officials acknowledged that torture and coerced confessions were chronic problems, they did not take sufficient measures to end these practices. Former detainees reported credibly that officials used electric shocks, prolonged periods of solitary confinement, incommunicado detention, beatings, shackles, and other forms of abuse. Recommendations from the May 2000 report of the UN Committee against Torture still had not been fully implemented by year's end. These recommendations included incorporating a definition of torture into domestic law, abolishing all forms of administrative detention (including reeducation through labor), promptly investigating all allegations of torture, and providing training courses on international human rights standards for police. During the year, police use of torture to coerce confessions from criminal suspects continued to be a problem. The 2002 death in custody of Zeng Lingyun of Chongqing Municipality remained unresolved. On July 26, 2002, public security personnel detained Zeng on theft charges. On July 28, his family was informed that he had died. Local officials initially told Zeng's family that he had been shot by police, and the family noticed extensive bruises and a bullet wound on the body. Since the crackdown on Falun Gong began in 1999, there reportedly have been several hundred deaths in custody of Falun Gong adherents, due to torture, abuse, and neglect.[41]

In the Philippines a similar picture emerges:

> The Constitution prohibits torture, and evidence obtained through its use is inadmissible in court; however, members of the security forces and police continued to use torture and to abuse suspects and detainees. The CHR [Commission on Human Rights] provides the police with mandatory human rights training, including primers on the rights of suspects, and higher level PNP [Philippine National Police] officials seemed more receptive to respecting the human rights of detainees; however, rank-and-file awareness of the rights of detainees remained inadequate.
>
> TFDP [The nongovernmental organization Task Force Detainees of the Philippines] stated that torture remained an ingrained part of the arrest and detention process. Common forms of abuse during arrest and interrogation reportedly included striking detainees and threatening them with guns. Less common forms included the placing of plastic bags over heads to deprive the detainee of air. TFDP reported that arresting officers often carried out such beatings in the early stages of detention.[42]

The United States in Iraq, Afghanistan, and Guantánamo Bay

The United States has also been widely engaged in the practice of torture in the context of the "war against terrorism." In 2004, graphic photographs of the torture of Iraqi prisoners occurring at Abu Ghraib spread around the world.[43] The photographs show prisoners bound in painful positions, placed in stress positions, such as being made to stand with arms outstretched, and forced into sexually humiliating positions.[44] Other abuses, reported by Major General Antonio Taguba in a secret report in March 2004, included pouring cold water on naked prisoners, beating inmates with a broom handle and chair, threats of rape, sodomy with a chemical light, using dogs to frighten and intimidate detainees, and forcing detainees to engage in sexually humiliating conduct, such as being arranged in "sexually explicit positions for photographing."[45]

In addition to the widely publicized photographs of torture occurring at the Abu Ghraib facility in Baghdad, Amnesty International, the International Committee of the Red Cross, and a variety of other commentators have reported numerous other instances of torture by United States personnel since the beginning of the "war on terror." Instances of torture have been reported primarily in Afghanistan, Iraq, and Guantánamo Bay, suggesting that the Abu Ghraib incidents were not merely isolated cases.[46] Among other case studies, Amnesty cites the treatment of Khreisan Khalis Aballey, who was arrested at his home in Baghdad in April 2003. Amnesty claims that:

> [d]uring his interrogation at Baghdad's airport detention facility, he was made to stand or kneel facing a wall for seven-and-a-half days, hooded, and handcuffed tightly. . . . At the same time, a bright light was placed next to his hood whilst distorted music was played. Throughout this period, he was deprived of sleep and fell unconscious some of the time. He reported that at one time a U.S. soldier stamped on his foot, tearing off one of his toenails. The prolonged kneeling made his knees bloody.[47]

In another case in April 2003, Abdallah Khudhran al-Shamran was reported to have been subjected to beatings and electric shocks as well as other torture methods, including sleep deprivation through the constant playing of loud music and "being suspended from his legs and having his penis tied."[48]

Even domestically, and prior to the "war on terror," the UN Committee against Torture claimed that American police officers and prison guards had engaged in various forms of torture and ill treatment on numerous occasions.[49] Of particular concern was the use of electroshock stun belts to restrain prisoners.[50] In addition, the United States has been repeatedly accused of turning over prisoners to other countries to have them tortured.[51] One official said, "We don't kick the [expletive] out of them. We send them to other countries so they can kick the [expletive] out of them."[52] In terms of the prevalence of torture in the United States, Dershowitz has noted:

> Many of the countries who are signatories to the various conventions routinely torture. . . . Egypt, Jordan and the Philippines are signatories—we know those countries torture. How do we know? Because the United States sends our detainees to those countries to have them tortured. Hypocrisy is prevailing today. My suggestion is that if the United States were to authorize torture, we would have to write a letter to the various signatory organizations saying we reserve the right under the convention to exclude the following from the definition of torture . . . and then we'd list our exceptions.[53]

It is easy to provide further examples of torture,[54] but enough has been said to emphasize the distinction between reality and rhetoric regarding torture.

CHAPTER THREE

The Moral Status of Torture

OVERVIEW

Broadly, there are two types of normative moral theories. Consequential moral theories claim that an act is right or wrong depending upon its capacity to maximize a particular virtue, such as happiness. Nonconsequential (or deontological) theories claim that the appropriateness of an action is not contingent upon its instrumental ability to produce particular ends, but rather follows from the intrinsic features of the act. Thus, the notion of absolute (or near absolute) rights, which now dominates moral discourse, is generally thought to sit most comfortably in a nonconsequentialist ethic.

It is argued that torture is permissible pursuant to both of these ethical theories. It is only consequentialist theories, however, that provide a logical framework within which it is possible to demarcate the circumstances in which torture is permissible.

Prior to discussing how torture sits in the context of these theories, an overview of the essential aspects of each of the theories is first discussed.

NONCONSEQUENTIALIST RIGHTS-BASED THEORIES

The main argument in support of rights-based moral theories is aptly stated by John Rawls, who claims that only rights-based theories take seriously the distinctive interests of individuals and protect certain rights and interests that are so paramount that they are beyond the demands of net happiness.[1]

The Proliferation of Rights Talk

Arguments of this type have been extremely influential. Following World War II, there has been an immense increase in rights talk,[2] both in sheer volume and the number of supposed rights. The rights doctrine has progressed a long way since its original modest aim of providing "a legitimization of . . . claims against tyrannical or exploiting regimes."[3] As Tom Campbell points out:

> The human rights movement is based on the need for a counter-ideology to combat the abuses and misuses of political authority by those who invoke, as a justification for their activities, the need to subordinate the particular interests of individuals to the general good.[4]

There is now, more than ever, a strong tendency to advance moral claims and arguments in terms of rights.[5] Assertion of rights has become the customary means to express moral sentiments: "There is virtually no area of public controversy in which rights are not to be found on at least one side of the question—and generally on both."[6] There is no question that "the doctrine of human rights has at least temporarily replaced the doctrine of maximizing utilitarianism as the prime philosophical inspiration of political and social reform."[7]

The influence of rights-based theories is demonstrated by the sheer number of international human rights instruments that most nations have signed or ratified. The main three of such instruments are the Universal Declaration of Human Rights, the International Covenant on Economic, Social, and Cultural Rights, and the International Covenant on Civil and Political Rights. There are dozens of rights that are prescribed in one form or another by at least one of these documents. The scope of these rights includes what can be described as basic protections, such as the right to life,[8] liberty, and security of person,[9] and to be free from torture or cruel, inhuman, or degrading treatment or punishment.[10] There are also the somewhat more vague rights, such as the right to the economic, social, and cultural rights that are said to be indispensable to one's dignity and the free development of one's personality.[11] Other such rights include the right to be free from the arbitrary interference with one's privacy, family, home, or correspondence and from attacks upon one's honor and reputation.[12] Then there are some so-called rights that are probably best placed on a wish list, such as the right to rest and leisure[13] and the right to a standard of living adequate for the health and well being of oneself and one's family, including food, clothing, housing, and medical care and necessary social services.[14]

Influential Contemporary Rights Theorists

Numerous rights-based theories have been advanced as a result of the colossal, and apparently ever-increasing, amount of ethical language that is expressed in the form of rights. Rights talk transcends all areas of moral discourse. Rights are now the conventional moral currency. The main differences between them are typically the precise rights that are acclaimed, the basis of the rights, and the absolutism with which they apply. The main role of rights in deontological theories is to protect people from being compelled to do something against their wishes for the good of another or the general good. Two of the most influential contemporary rights theories are examined in the following sections—those of Ronald Dworkin and Robert Nozick. Many of the observations made in relation to these theories are applicable to most other rights-based theories.

Dworkin: Concern and Respect

For Dworkin, rights are "political trumps held by individuals,"[15] which protect them from the pursuit of common goods.

Dworkin states that "[t]he prospect of utilitarian gains cannot justify preventing a man from doing what he has a right to do,"[16] and that the general good is never an adequate basis for limiting rights.[17] He asserts that people have rights when there are good reasons for conferring upon them benefits or opportunities despite a community interest to the contrary.[18]

According to Dworkin, in order to take rights seriously, one

> must accept . . . one or both of two important ideas. The first is the vague but powerful idea of human dignity. This idea, associated with Kant . . . supposes that there are ways of treating a man that are inconsistent with recognizing him as a full member of the human community, and holds that such treatment is profoundly unjust.

The second is the more familiar idea of political equality.[19]

Observance of these ideals leads to the fundamental right of equal concern and respect, which is the foundation of Dworkin's rights thesis.[20] Under this theory, it makes sense to say that a person has a right if that right is necessary to protect the person's dignity or his standing as being equally entitled to concern and respect. To treat one with concern is to treat one as a human being, capable of suffering and frustration,[21] and to accord respect is to recognize one as a human being capable of forming and acting on intelligent conceptions of how life should be lived.[22]

Nozick: Rights that Exist in a State of Nature

Robert Nozick's rights theory stems from his analysis of the legitimate role of the state.[23] For the purpose of this discussion, the end product of this state is less important than Nozick's picture of morality that underpins it. Nozick believes that morality is founded on rights. For him, the rights we have are those that supposedly exist in a state of nature and derive from our natural liberty.[24] This gives rise to several distinct rights: the right to absolute control over ourselves, the right to be free from all forms of physical violations, and the right to acquire property and other resources as a result of the proper exercise of our personal rights. These rights are contingent upon not violating the same rights of others. Individuals also have the right to exact retribution against, and compensation from, those who violate their rights. Under this theory, moral rights are said to act as side constraints on the actions of others and cannot be violated even to achieve greater goods.[25] Thus, on Nozick's account, moral rights are negative rights—there are no positive rights such as the right to welfare or health care.[26]

On the basis of either theory, torture is on its face offensive. For Dworkin, torture does not accord an agent the concern and respect that is owed to each individual. For Nozick, torture is indefensible because it directly violates the right to be free from physical violations.

The Emptiness of Rights Theories and Application of Rights Theories to the Terrorist-plane Scenario

Despite the dazzling veneer of deontological rights-based theories and their influence on present-day moral and legal discourse, when examined closely, such theories are unable to provide persuasive answers to central issues such as: What is the justification for rights? How can we distinguish real from fanciful rights? Which right takes priority in the event of conflicting rights?[27] Such intractable difficulties stem from the fact that contemporary rights theories lack a coherent foundation for rights. Tom Campbell has argued against certain rights-based theories on the basis that they are unable to provide a satisfactory account of the relationship between concrete rights (rights that provide a justification for political decisions by society in general) and more fundamental rights ("background rights") from which concrete rights are supposedly derived.[28] However, an even more fundamental flaw with rights theories is that there is no defensible virtue that underpins the background interests from which narrower rights claims can be derived.

When examined closely, the concept of nonconsequentialist rights is vacuous at the epistemological level. It has been argued that attempts to ground concrete rights in virtues such as dignity, integrity, concern, and respect are unsound because they resort to such ideals is arbitrary and leads to discrimination against certain members of the community (for example, those with severely limited cognitive functioning) or speciesism (the systematic discrimination against nonhumans).[29]

Ultimately, a nonconsequentialist ethic provides no method for distinguishing between genuine and fanciful rights claims and is incapable of providing guidance regarding the ranking of rights in the event of a clash. It is not surprising then that nowadays all sorts of dubious rights claims have been advanced. Thus, we have a situation where individuals are able to hold a straight face and urge interests such as "the right to a tobacco-free job," the "right to sunshine," the "right of a father to be present in the delivery room," the "right to a sex break,"[30] and even the "right to drink myself to death without interference."[31]

A further flaw with many rights theories, including those of Dworkin and Nozick, is that an absolute right does not exist. Not even the right to life is sacrosanct. This is evident from the fact that all cultures sanction the use of lethal force in self-defense. And, indeed, torture in the circumstances that we indicate is morally permissible, is in fact a manifestation of the right to self-defense, which extends to the right to defend another. By conceding that in some situations consequences must prevail, Dworkin's and Nozick's respective theories become unstable.

Despite the absolute overtones of their theories and their insistence of the importance of the individual, Dworkin and Nozick would probably, yet reluctantly, respond to the terrorist-plane example and the Osama bin Laden hostage scenario by approving of torture in those circumstances.

Dworkin accepts that it is correct for a government to infringe on a right when it is necessary to protect a more important right or to ward off "some grave threat to society."[32] In like manner, Nozick states that teleological considerations would take over to "avert moral catastrophe."[33] Although both fail to state, even loosely, at what point a great threat to society or a moral catastrophe exists, so that consequentialist considerations can legitimately "kick in" to guide conduct, it is tenable to argue that the loss of many innocent lives satisfies this criteria.

When consequential considerations are admitted as being relevant, the theories become hybrid and the main theoretical advantage of a deontological theory, the absolute protection given to people against certain intrusions, is forsaken. This problem is heightened because, in both cases, we are given no guidance as to when consequentialist considerations become overriding. At this point rights theories collapse—they cannot rely fully on the theoretical justifications of deontological or consequentialist theories.

More than twenty years ago, Hart said of rights theories, "It cannot be said that we have had . . . a sufficiently detailed or adequately articulate theory showing the foundation for such rights and how they are related to other values . . . Indeed the revived doctrines of basic rights . . . are in spite of much brilliance still unconvincing."[34]

Nothing has changed to diminish the force of this objection.

This may seem to be unduly dismissive of rights-based theories and to pay inadequate regard to the considerable moral reforms that have occurred against the backdrop of rights talk over the past half-century. It cannot be denied that rights claims have been an effective lever for social change. Campbell correctly notes that rights have provided "a constant source of inspiration for the protection of individual liberty rights."[35] For example, recognition of the right to liberty resulted in the abolition of slavery and, more recently, the right of equality has been used as an effective weapon by women and other disempowered groups seeking greater employment and civil rights, such as the right to vote.

There is no doubt that there is an ongoing need for moral discourse in the form of rights; "[w]hether or not . . . rights are intellectually defensible or culturally tolerant, we do have need of them, at least at the edges of civilization and in the tangle of international politics."[36] Rather, as is discussed below, the only manner in which rights can be substantiated is in the context of a consequentialist ethic. The criticism is with *deontological* rights-based moral theories and their absolutist overtones. Theories of this nature are incapable of providing answers to questions such as the existence and content of proposed rights. This view could obviously be criticized on the basis that if nonconsequentialist rights are fanciful, then one has difficulty accounting for the significant changes to the moral landscape for which they have provided the catalyst.

There are several responses to this. First, the fact that a belief or judgment is capable of moving and guiding human conduct says little about its truth—the widespread practice of burning "witches" being a case in point. Second, at the descriptive level, it is probably the case that the intuitive appeal of rights claims and the absolutist and forceful manner in which they are expressed has been normally sufficient to mask over fundamental logical deficiencies associated with the concept of rights. Claims couched in the language of rights seem to carry more emotive punch than equivalent claims grounded in the language of duties. For whatever reason (perhaps due to the egocentric nature of rights discourse) the claim that "I have a right to life" appears to resonate more powerfully than the assertion that "you have a duty not to kill me." In effect, the much-criticized[37] meta-ethical theory of emotivism, which provides that morality is a set of utterances that express one's attitude with the aim of influencing the behavior of others, seems to provide at least a partial explanation for the influence of rights-based discourse.

TORTURE AND UTILITARIANISM

There has been a range of consequentialist moral theories advanced, such as egoism and utilitarianism. The most cogent of these theories, and certainly the most influential in moral and political discourse, is hedonistic act utilitarianism. This theory provides that the morally right action is that which produces the greatest amount of happiness or pleasure and the least amount of pain or unhappiness.[38]

Utilitarianism has received a lot of bad press over the past few decades,[39] resulting in its demise as the leading normative theory. There are several reasons for this. The main general argument against utilitarianism is that because it prioritizes net happiness over individual pursuits, it fails to safeguard fundamental individual interests. As a result of this, it has been argued that in some circumstances utilitarianism leads to horrendous outcomes, such as punishing the innocent[40] or forcing organ donations where the donations would maximize happiness by saving the lives of many or assisting those most in need.[41] These outcomes are essentially inflicting harsh pain on one person for the benefit of others. Another major criticism of utilitarianism is that it supposedly does not accord sufficient weight to individual interests. As noted above, it has been charged that only rights-based theories take seriously the distinction between human beings. This is in contrast to utilitarianism, where the ultimate goal—happiness—is aggregative in nature. The happiness of any particular individual is trumped by the goal of net human happiness.

Against a background of utilitarian ethic, torture is clearly justifiable where the harm caused to the agent will be offset by the increased happiness gained to other people.[42] Utilitarianism has been persuasively criticized in the eyes of many, precisely because it justifies supposedly egregious conduct of this nature. Thus, it can be argued that the fact that utilitarianism justifies torture indicates that the theory is flawed. Historically, the same sort of argument has been used most forcefully in the context that utilitarianism may justify punishing the innocent.

A famous illustration of the objection concerning punishing the innocent is McCloskey's small-town sheriff example:

> Suppose a sheriff were faced with the choice of either framing a negro for a rape which had aroused white hostility to negroes (this particular negro being believed to be guilty) and thus preventing serious anti-negro riots which would probably lead to loss of life, or of allowing the riots to occur. If he were . . . [a] utilitarian he would be committed to framing the negro.[43]

Hard Cases Lead to Hard Decisions

A common utilitarian response to this dilemma is that such examples are impossible in the real world and hence need not be addressed.[44] Punishing the innocent may at times provide short-term benefits, such as securing social stability. Nevertheless, these benefits are always more than offset by the likelihood of greater long-term harm due to the loss of confidence in the legal system and the associated loss of security to all members of the community who will fear that they may be the next person framed, once the inevitable occurs and it is disclosed that an innocent person has been punished. But with only a little imagination, the above example can be tightened up by introducing considerations that significantly reduce or totally obviate the possibility of disclosure, so that the only logical utilitarian conclusion is to punish the innocent.[45] Even if the process of modifying the examples appears to far remove them from the real world, it is still a situation that the utilitarian must deal with.

The more promising utilitarian response is not to attempt to deflect or avoid the conclusion that there may be some extreme situations where utilitarianism commits us to punishing the innocent or torturing individuals, but rather the correct approach is to accept this outcome and contend that, as horrible as this may seem on a prereflective level, on closer consideration it is not a matter that *really* insurmountably troubles our sensibilities to the extent that it entails that any theory that approves of such an outcome must necessarily be flawed. By drawing comparisons with other situations in which we take the utilitarian option, it is contended that practices such as punishing the innocent and torture are not necessarily unacceptable.

The view that punishing the innocent and torturing individuals is the morally correct action in some circumstances is consistent with and accords with the decisions we as individuals and societies as a whole readily have made and continue to make when faced with extreme and desperate circumstances. Once we come to grips with the fact that our decisions in extreme situations will be compartmentalized to desperate predicaments, we do, and *should*, though perhaps somewhat begrudgingly, take the utilitarian option. In the face of extreme situations, we are quite ready to accept that one should, or even must, sacrifice oneself or *others* for the good of the whole. The need to make such decisions is of course regrettable, but more regrettable still would be not making them and thereby increasing net human pain.

For example, in times of war we not only request our strongest and healthiest to fight to the death for the good of the community, but we often demand that they do so under threat of imprisonment or even death. Quite often they must battle against hopeless odds, in circumstances where we are aware that in all probability they are not coming back.[46] What is more: they *must* give their life. Not because they want to, not because they are bad, but merely because it would be good for the rest of us. This is classical utilitarian reasoning. Faced with the reality of the decisions we *do* make in such horrible situations, the examples proffered against utilitarianism about the terrible things it entails, such as punishing the innocent, lose their bite.

Horrible situations make for appalling decisions whichever way we turn, but ultimately we do make the utilitarian choice because of our lack of true commitment to any higher moral virtue. By opting for the utilitarian line we are soothed by one saving grace: at least the level of harm has been minimized. When the good of many or the whole is at significant threat, we have no difficulty selecting certain classes of innocent individuals, whose only "flaw" is their sex, state of health, and date of birth to go in to bat for the rest of us. Their protests that they should not be compelled to go because it impinges on their civil, legal, or human rights to such matters as life and liberty, or their desperate appeals to other virtues such as justice or integrity, fall on obstinate ears; for this is serious stuff now—our lives (or other important interests) are at stake. Such appeals should be saved for rosier times. When advanced in theory, we can all "agree" that this is so.

The decisions we do actually make in a real-life crisis are the best evidence of the way we actually do prioritize important, competing principles and interests. Matters such as rights and justice are important, but, in the end, are subservient to, and make way for, the ultimate matter of significance: general happiness. Bad as it seems, framing the African American and imprisoning the innocent, and torturing the terrorist are certainly no more horrendous than the decisions history has shown we have made in circumstances of monumental crisis.

A pointed example is the decision by then-English Prime Minister Winston Churchill to sacrifice the lives of the residents of Coventry in order to not alert the Germans that the English had deciphered German radio messages. On November 14, 1940, the English decoded plans that the Germans were about to air bomb Coventry.[47] If Coventry had been evacuated or its inhabitants advised to take special precautions against the raid, the Germans would have known that their code had been cracked, and the English would have been unable to obtain future information about the intentions of its enemy.[48] Churchill elected not to warn the citizens of Coventry, and many hundreds were killed in the raid that followed. Many innocent lives were sacrificed in order not to reveal the secret that would hopefully save many more lives in the future.[49] Significantly, such decisions (and other similar examples discussed in chapter 7) have subsequently been immune from widespread or persuasive criticism. This shows not only that when pressed we *do* take the utilitarian option, but also that it is felt that this is the option we *should* take. In chapter 7 further examples are given that emphasize this point.

Now, what we actually do does not justify what ought to be done. Morality is normative, not descriptive, in nature: an "ought" cannot be derived from an "is."[50] Nevertheless, the above analysis is telling because the force of the "punishing the innocent" objection lies in the fact that it supposedly so troubles our moral consciousness that utilitarianism can thereby be dismissed because the outcome is so horrible that "there must be a mistake somewhere." But this claim loses its force when it is shown that punishing the innocent and torturing the culpable is, in fact, no worse than other activities that we condone.

The Role of Rights in a Utilitarian Ethic

The criticism that utilitarianism has no place for rights must be responded to for the sake of completeness (and in an attempt to further redeem utilitarianism). Rights do in fact have a place in a utilitarian ethic, and, what is more, it is only against this background that rights can be explained and their source justified. Utilitarianism provides a sounder foundation for rights than any other competing theory. Indeed, for the utilitarian, the answer to why rights exist is simple: recognition of them best promotes general utility.[51] Their origin accordingly lies in the pursuit of happiness.[52] Their content is discovered through empirical observations regarding the patterns of behavior that best advance the utilitarian cause. The long association of utilitarianism and rights appears to have been forgotten by most. However, more than a century ago it was Mill who proclaimed the right of free speech, contending that truth is important to the attainment of general happiness and this is best discovered by its competition with falsehood.[53]

There is a place for rights in a utilitarian theory because difficulties in performing the utilitarian calculus regarding each decision make it desirable that we ascribe certain rights and interests to people that evidence shows tend to maximize happiness[54]—even more happiness than if we made all of our decisions without such guidelines. Rights save time and energy by serving as shortcuts to assist us in attaining desirable consequences. By labeling certain interests as rights, we are spared the tedious task of establishing the importance of a particular interest as a first premise in practical arguments.[55] There are also other reasons why performing the utilitarian calculus on each occasion may be counterproductive to the ultimate aim. Our capacity to gather and process information and our foresight are restricted by a large number of factors, including lack of time, indifference to the matter at hand, defects in reasoning, and so on. We are quite often not in a good position to assess all the possible alternatives and to determine the likely impact upon general happiness stemming from each alternative. Our ability to make the correct decision will be greatly assisted if we can narrow down the range of relevant factors in light of predetermined guidelines. History has shown that certain patterns of conduct and norms of behavior, if observed, are most conducive to promoting happiness. These observations are given expression in the form of rights that can be asserted in the absence of evidence as to why adherence to them in the particular case would not maximize net happiness.

Thus, rights in a utilitarian view do not have a life of their own (they are derivative, not foundational), as is the case with deontological theories. Due to the derivative character of utilitarian rights, they do not carry the same degree of absolutism or "must be doneness" as those based on deontological theories. However, this is not a drawback of utilitarianism but a strength, because it is farcical to claim that any right is absolute. Another advantage of utilitarianism is that only it provides a mechanism for ranking rights and other interests. In the event of a clash, the victor is the right that will generate the most happiness. As the next part discusses, the balancing aspect of utilitarianism is the reason that it is particularly apposite to determining the circumstances in which torture is appropriate.

THE CIRCUMSTANCES IN WHICH
TORTURE IS ACCEPTABLE

The only situation where torture is justifiable is where it is used as an information-gathering technique to avert a grave risk. In such circumstances, there are five variables relevant in determining whether torture is permissible and the degree of torture that is appropriate. The variables are (1) the number of lives at risk; (2) the immediacy of the harm; (3) the availability of other means to acquire the information; (4) the level of wrongdoing of the agent; and (5) the likelihood that the agent actually does possess the relevant information. Where (1), (2), (4), and (5) rate highly and (3) is low, all forms of harm may be inflicted on the agent—although the aim is to inflict the minimum degree of harm necessary to obtain the relevant information.

The Harm to Be Prevented

The key consideration regarding the permissibility of torture is the magnitude of harm that is sought to be prevented. To this end, the appropriate measure is the number of lives that are likely to be lost if the threatened harm is not averted. Obviously, the more lives that are at stake, the more weight that is attributed to this variable.

Lesser forms of threatened harm will not justify torture. Logically, the right to life is the most basic and fundamental of all human rights—nonobservance of it would render all other human rights devoid of meaning.[56] Every society has some prohibition against taking life,[57] and "the intentional taking of human life is . . . the offense which society condemns most strongly."[58] The right to life is also enshrined in several international covenants. For example, Article 2 of the European Convention on Human Rights (which in essence mirrors Article 6 of the International Covenant on Civil and Political Rights) provides that "everyone's right to life shall be protected by law. No one shall be deprived of his life intentionally save in the execution of a sentence of a court following his conviction of a crime for which this penalty is provided by law."[59]

Torture violates the right to physical integrity, which is so important that it is only a threat to the right to life that can justify interference with it. Thus, torture should be confined to situations where the right to life is imperiled.

Immediacy of Harm and Other Options to Obtain Information

Torture should only be used as a last resort and hence should not be used where there is time to pursue other avenues of forestalling the harm. It is for this reason that torture should only be used where there is no other means to obtain the relevant information. Thus, where a terrorist has planted a bomb on a plane, torture will not be permissible where, for example, videotapes of international airports are likely to reveal the location of the plane that has been targeted.

When it is used, the minimum degree of pain necessary should be used to obtain the information. In particular, means that inflict long-term injury should be avoided.

Admittedly, sometimes the level of pain involved will be very high, thereby even risking the death of a suspect—as result of the "thin skull" conundrum (we can never predict with absolute certainty how people will cope with severe pain). The intentional killing of a suspect is never justified, however. No information can be gathered after a suspect is dead. Moreover, the death of a suspect would significantly add to the antitorture side of the utilitarian calculus.

These considerations should not be made public, otherwise some subjects of torture would have an incentive to hold out, knowing that there are limits to the amount of pain that might be inflicted on them.

An Important Consideration is the Likelihood of Knowledge or Guilt

As a general rule, torture should normally be confined to people who are responsible in some way for the threatened harm. However, this is not invariably the case. People who are simply aware of the threatened harm, that is, "innocent people," may in some circumstances also be subjected to torture.

It should be noted that people who have information that can save many lives, if questioned, are morally required to provide the information. It would be morally wrong for them to decline to do so, for the same reasons that it is wrong for a person to refuse to save a baby drowning in a puddle. Thus, they are not innocent in a moral sense. This is the same rationale that is used to justify the policy, which is discussed further in chapter 6, in all common law countries that requires witnesses to criminal acts to give evidence (under the threat of imprisonment) in court cases when subpoenaed to do so.

Regardless of the guilt of the agent, it is most important that torture is only used against individuals who actually possess the relevant information. It will be rare that conclusive proof is available that an individual does, in fact, possess the required knowledge; for example, potential torturees will not have been through a trial process in which their guilt has been established. However, this is not a decisive objection to the use of torture. The investigation and trial process is simply one means of distinguishing wrongdoers from the innocent. To that end, it does not seem to be a particularly effective process. There are other ways of forming such conclusions. One is by way of lie-detector tests. The latest information suggests that polygraphs are accurate about 80 to 90 percent of the time.[60] There has been little empirical research done to ascertain the number of innocent people who are ultimately convicted of criminal offenses. However, as one example, research carried out in the United Kingdom for the Royal Commission on Criminal Justice suggests that up to 11 percent of people who plead guilty claim innocence.[61] The wrongful acquittal rate would no doubt be even higher than this.

Moreover, it is important to note that even without resort to polygraphs there will be many circumstances where guilt or relevant knowledge is patently obvious. A clear example is where a person makes a relevant admission that discloses information that would only be within the knowledge of the wrongdoer. Another example occurred in the recent German kidnapping case, referred to earlier, where the man in custody had been witnessed collecting a ransom and had indicated to the police that the kidnapped boy was still alive.[62] Where lesser forms of evidence proving guilt are available, the argument in favor of torture is lower.

The Formula

Incorporating all these considerations, the strength of the case in favor of torture can be mapped as follows:

$$\frac{W \times L \times P}{T \times O}$$

Where:

W = whether the agent is the wrongdoer

L = the number of lives that will be lost if the information is not provided

P = the probability that the agent has the relevant knowledge

T = the time available before the disaster will occur ("immediacy of the harm")

O = the likelihood that other inquiries will forestall the risk

W is a weighting that is attributable to whether the agent has had any direct connection with the potential catastrophe. Where the person is responsible for the incident (for example, planted or organized the bomb), this variable will apply more strongly. Where the agent is innocent and has simply stumbled on the relevant information (for example, he or she saw the bomb being planted or overheard the plan to plant the bomb), this should be reduced by a certain amount.

Torture should be permitted where the application of the variables exceeds a threshold level. Once beyond this level, the higher the figure, the more severe the forms of torture that are permissible. There is no bright line that can be drawn concerning the point at which the "torture threshold" should be set.

There is obviously a degree of imprecision attached to this process and considerable scope for discussion and disagreement regarding the *exact* weight that should be attached to each variable. It is important to emphasize, however, that this is not an argument against the proposal. Many legal standards include nonnumerical criteria and employ notions such as reasonableness, proportionality, and immediacy (for example, the notion of self-defense). The above criteria for the use of torture are more pointed than many existing legal tests and hence there is no basis for believing that torture will be sanctioned in inappropriate circumstances.

In addition to the moral argument for torture (as an interrogation device), Dershowitz has argued that torture should be legalized for harm-minimization reasons. Dershowitz has pushed for the introduction of "a torture warrant," which would place a "heavy burden on the government to demonstrate by factual evidence the necessity to administer this horrible, horrible technique of torture."[63] He further adds:

> I think that we're much, much better off admitting what we're doing or not doing it at all. I agree with you, it will much better if we never did it. But if we're going to do it and subcontract and find ways of circumventing, it's much better to do what Israel did. They were the only country in the world ever directly to confront the issue, and it led to a supreme court decision, as you say, outlawing torture, and yet Israel has been criticized all over the world for confronting the issue directly. Candor and accountability in a democracy is very important. Hypocrisy has no place.[64]

The main advantage with requiring a warrant is that the legality of coercive interrogation techniques would be assessed before the act, as opposed to being retrospectively judged after the event. As we shall see in chapter 8, the law of necessity would already permit torture in the circumstances outlined above.

Thus, we have seen that the absolute prohibition against torture is morally unsound and pragmatically unworkable. There is a need for measured discussion regarding the merits of torture as an information-gathering device. This would result in the legal use of torture in circumstances where there are a large number of lives at risk in the immediate future and there is no other means of alleviating the threat. While none of the recent high-profile cases of torture appear to satisfy these criteria, it is likely that circumstances will arise in the future where torture is legitimate and desirable. A legal framework should be established to properly accommodate these situations.

In the next four chapters we consider the counterarguments that have been advanced against our proposal.

CHAPTER FOUR

The Slippery Slope Illusion

OVERVIEW OF CRITICISMS OF LIFE-SAVING TORTURE

As noted in the preface, our suggestion that life-saving torture is morally permissible provoked widespread debate and many criticisms. It is not feasible to respond to all of the criticisms. In the next four chapters we address the most persuasive and pervasive criticisms that have been levelled against our position.

By way of overview, there were four main attacks on our position. The first is the slippery slope or thin edge of wedge argument. If torture is condoned in the circumstances we set out it will supposedly result in the widespread use of torture. Secondly, and related to this point, is that legalizing torture will dehumanize society.

A more pragmatic objection to our proposal is that torture does not work. Suspects that are tortured will, supposedly, not "fess up." This is the third main line of criticism. The fourth point made by some critics is that legalization of torture would be "antidemocratic."

We now consider the response in that order.

OVERVIEW OF SLIPPERY SLOPE ARGUMENT

The slippery slope or the dangerous precedent argument (also often run under the banners of "thin end of the wedge," "the tip of the iceberg," or the "floodgates argument") has loomed large in this debate.[1]

"If you start opening the door, making a little exception here, a little exception there, you've basically sent the signal that the ends justify the means," resulting in even more torture.[2] The slippery slope argument is often invoked in relation to acts that in themselves are justified, but which have similarities with objectionable practices, and urges that in morally appraising an action we must not only consider its intrinsic features but also the likelihood of it being used as a basis for condoning similar, but in fact relevantly different, undesirable practices.[3]

Thus, if our proposal for limited torture is accepted, the critics argue that it will lead to the greater use of torture—extending well beyond the narrow parameters of life-saving torture.

This slippery slope criticism is a distraction in this debate. It deflects attention from our actual proposal and diverts readers to profoundly immoral forms of torture. There is no demonstrated connection between the two practices other than the inventive imagination of the critics.

Proposals cannot be rebutted merely by stating that acceptance of them *might* lead to bad outcomes because it might lead to similar undesirable practices. If this were the case, even unquestionably desirable practices would be thwarted. For example, the suggestion that we should donate more to the developing world to feed the 16,000 children who starve daily[4] could be rebutted by a retort that it might lead the starving world down the slippery slope of relying on handouts (instead of being self-sufficient).

Slopes, wedges, icebergs, and floods cannot be plucked out on a whim. They need to be constructed or at least verified.

This is not to say that the slippery slope argument is always a fallacy. The slippery slope argument has been criticized on the basis that it logically prevents change and advancement. It has been suggested that it amounts to the proposition that:

You should not now do an admittedly right action for
fear that you . . . should not have the courage to do the

right thing in some future case, which ex hypothesis is essentially different, but superficially resembles the present one. Every public action which is not customary either is wrong, or, if it is right, is a dangerous precedent. It follows that nothing should ever be done for the first time.[5]

We do not accept this. It fails to recognize the real force behind the slippery slope argument, which lies in our propensity to justify new practices by analogizing from one situation to another, and our fallibility in discerning the relevant and significant factors about the practices we are comparing. But use of the slippery slope argument to be valid must be sharply focused. To this end, there are two versions of the slippery slope argument: the logical and the empirical.

The logical form of the argument is the view that clear boundaries cannot be drawn around the practice under consideration. In the context of life-saving torture, this form of the argument is unconvincing. The *reasons* advanced in favor of life-saving torture, namely the compassionate desire to save innocent life, are clear and pointed considerations. A bright line can be drawn between using torture as a last resort to save innocent lives and using torture as an act of suppression, domination, or cruelty.

The empirical version of the slippery slope argument provides that if torture is condoned in any circumstances, it will as a matter of fact lead to a greater preparedness to use it in other circumstances where it is not justifiable. This argument is also flawed.

THE TORTURE FLOODGATES HAVE BURST

First, the floodgates are already open—torture is widely used, despite the absolute legal prohibition against it. It is, in fact, arguable that it is the existence of an unrealistic absolute ban on torture that has driven torture "beneath the radar screen of accountability,"[6] and that the legalization of torture in very rare circumstances would, in fact, reduce its use because of the increased level of accountability.[7] Given that there are reports of torture and ill-treatment from 132 countries, including the United States, Canada, and France it is not clear that there is meaningful scope for the practice of torture to increase.

The absolute prohibition on torture is no doubt part of the reason that the United States engages in rendition, which consists of apprehending, detaining, transporting, and interrogating terrorist suspects outside the United States, where the suspects cannot avail themselves of the normal prohibition that applies in relation to cruel forms of interrogation. In December 2005, U.S. Secretary of State Condoleeza Rice conceded that U.S. intelligence agencies transport detainees to other countries for coercive questioning—although she denied that the interrogation was so coercive as to constitute torture. These comments were made as the Bush administration came under criticism over allegations the CIA operates covert interrogation camps for terror suspects in several countries, including two in Eastern Europe.[8]

The practice of rendition is unacceptable largely because of the fact that it is totally unregulated. The justification is necessity—we supposedly need to get the information from the bad guys. If that is the case, we need to set the parameters for when this can occur. The absolute formal prohibition on torture inhibits open and considered discussion on this issue.

SLIPPERY SLOPES CANNOT BE INVENTED

Secondly, there is no evidence that life-saving torture will lead to violation of other rights where the preconditions for the practice are clearly delineated. Empirically based slippery slope arguments only obtain some traction where there is evidence that a practice similar to that being proposed has expanded beyond its intended scope of application after the practice was sanctioned. In order for the empirical version of the slippery slope argument to have a veneer of plausibility it is necessary to point to a situation where condoning life-saving torture has yielded widespread abuse. This is obviously too high a standard in the case at hand given that torture has never been legalized in the circumstances that we propose. The very least that can be expected in such cases is a close analogy, whereby a state-sanctioned practice that was founded on a desire to save innocent lives has resulted in large-scale abuses. There are no such analogies. In fact, the closest analogies to our proposal lead to the opposite conclusion.

The salient features of our proposal are (i) the motivation for the practice is compassion; (ii) it involves sacrificing a lower interest of one person to confer a greater benefit on another; (iii) it is almost certain that the suspect has the relevant information; and (iv) approval must be obtained from a state official (preferably a judge) before the activity can proceed.

While there are no institutionalized practices that have these precise four elements, there are some practices that come very close and none of them has resulted in widespread abuses. The closest parallel is live donor organ transplants. Elements (i) and (ii) are identical; the analogy with element (iii) is obvious given that in most cases we are almost certain that the organ will be a match and in relation to element (iv) in the place of a judge is a doctor.

Advances in medicine now make it possible to have procedures such as kidney and bone marrow transplants. These cause considerable pain to the donors, but confer a great benefit to the recipients. Less pain is caused by donating blood, but the underlying rationale is the same—hurting one person to benefit another. The practice of live donor transplants has not resulted in large-scale abuse. People are not plucked from the streets to have their organs plundered. Of course, the difference between this and our torture proposal is that the organ transfer process is consensual. This is not a relevant difference because nonconsensual practices based on the same rationales have also not lead to abuses.

To this end, a clear example is the process of criminal punishment. All nations imprison people who are regarded as being a risk to the community.[9] Some nations even kill their worst offenders. This institutionalized system of harm infliction has certainly resulted in some degree of abuse regarding the use of detention or state-sanctioned execution; however, in statistical terms abuses are relatively rare—certainly far less than the harm caused if we did not have a system for incarcerating wrongdoers.

Even laws that permit citizens to use self-help measures to inflict (even lethal) harm such as self-defense and necessity have not resulted in significant abuses. This is despite the fact that such laws are "gray" in application and the lawfulness of the conduct is generally evaluated after that fact.

The trend is all one way. Compassion-based laws that involve direct harm to one person for the benefit of another person or the wider community do not lead to widespread abuses. There is no reason to believe that the situation would be any different in relation to our proposal.

This is not to say that the empirical version of the slippery slope argument is always without foundation. In fact, one of us has relied on it heavily in the context of the voluntary euthanasia debate to argue that the practice should not be legalized in Western countries because it is likely to lead to abuses in the form of nonvoluntary euthanasia. This argument is based on wide-ranging data from the Western nation which has the longest tradition of legalizing euthanasia (the Netherlands), which showed that in a climate where voluntary euthanasia is permitted a large number of incidents of nonvoluntary euthanasia occur. The important aspect of this line of reasoning is that the slippery slope argument was not plucked out; rather, it was empirically grounded.[10] Of course there is scope to argue against the validity of the slippery slope theory in the euthanasia context. For example, it could be suggested that despite the apparent similarity between the Netherlands and many other Western nations there are in fact subtle (but relevant) unique social and cultural dynamics that exist in the Netherlands. Nevertheless, in the case of euthanasia a foundation for the slippery slope argument was laid. Not so in the case of the torture debate—here the critics have not got past the creative thinking stage.

So why is it that compassion-motivated practices that involve setting off the interests of one individual against those of another or the common good do not result in widespread abuses? There is no clear reason for this. But speculating, for one moment, we believe it is because most people seem to have a genuine dislike for the concept of harming others and, rightly, give less weight to speculative benefits than certain harms. We are never quite sure that the bone marrow transplant will work or that capital punishment or imprisonment are effective, but we are sure that they cause hardship to the donor and the wrongdoer. Thus, we tread warily when it comes to engaging in such practices. Rather than building slippery slopes, we erect increasingly high barriers to such practices. Such is likely to be the case with life-saving torture.

The critics have catalogued at great length past episodes of torture. They missed one elementary point. None of the abuses in places such as Guantanamo Bay, Algiers, Northern Ireland, Iraq (by Iraqi and U.S. forces), Greece, Israel[11] and any of the more than 100 or so other locations where torture has occurred were caused by a slide down the slippery slope from life-saving torture to torture for reasons of punishment and domination. These incidents of torture generally occurred against the backdrop of widespread hatred and anger in war or war-like situations where there was a suspension of even the most fundamental moral standards. Torture did not cause this. It was a symptom of the intense hatred that occurs when groups start killing each other for reasons such as race, land disputes, and religious differences. Alternatively, the cases of torture referred to by the critics relate to clandestine activities by misguided security officials "fishing" for information—the disanalogy with our proposal is evident.

Thus, in the context of the torture debate the only evidence of the slippery slope argument is that many of the critics have lost their intellectual balance and slid down the slope of placing undue reliance on the slippery slope argument.

CONCLUSION REGARDING SLIPPERY SLOPE ARGUMENT

The slippery slope argument, though probably the most common criticism of our proposal, is the easiest to rebut. Sometimes there are no slippery slopes or wedges with thin parts to be found and there is not even a trickle behind the floodgates. Such is the case with life-saving torture. There is no evidence to suggest that an institutionalized practice of inflicting pain on one person to save another or for the common good will lead to abuses. Capital punishment and kidney and bone marrow transplants illustrate this.

We condone torture only in one circumstance: as a means to save innocent lives. We condone it only for one reason: compassion. A framework based on these criteria has little prospect of being extended to encompass malevolent practices. The slippery slope argument is a distraction in the context of our proposal. Slippery slopes, thin-ended wedges, and icebergs with small tips cannot be plucked out of thin air to fill logical deficiencies in one's argument. They have to be verified and proven.

The slippery slope argument in the context of this debate is an illustration of intellectual sloppiness or expedience. The analysis is sloppy because the critics have failed to discern the salient aspects of the torture to save life proposal and thereby misrepresented where it might lead us to. Torture for compassionate reasons is no more an act of brutality than surgery to transplant a kidney from one person to save another person. That is the path we are going down, not brutalizing people out of hatred.

The slippery slope argument is an expedience in this debate because it is employed by some critics as a basis to avoid considering the *actual proposal* at hand (torture to save lives) and instead is used as a launching pad to embark on a nonresponsive dissertation about practices that have little connection with the proposal. Torture for life-saving purposes is far removed from any of the instances of the barbaric, punitive forms of torture mentioned by the critics. Yes, we all hate the thought of torture, but torture as has been practiced throughout history has at best a remote connection with our proposal.

CHAPTER FIVE

Life-saving Torture Is a Humane Practice

TORTURE WILL NOT DEHUMANIZE SOCIETY

The argument that condoning torture in any circumstances will brutalise or dehumanize[1] is flawed because it takes an unduly narrow perspective of the proposal at hand and mischaracterizes the motivation for the proposal.

It should be noted that this criticism is sometimes put as a stand-alone argument. On other occasions it is a premise of the slippery slope argument, along the lines that any torture will result in more torture because it will desensitize people to the suffering of others.

There is no doubt that inflicting pain on people is bad. In our view, the reduction of pain should be one of the highest-order moral imperatives. But there is no basis for ranking one person's pain more importantly than that of another. When we are confronted with a situation where we must chose between who will bear unavoidable pain, we need to take a pain-minimization approach. To this end, there is no question that causing (even intense) physical pain to a suspect causes less pain than allowing many people to be blown up. The enduring pain that would be felt by the relatives of the victims grossly outweighs the physical pain inflicted on the suspect.

In assessing the potential dehumanizing aspect of a proposal, there is no logical or moral basis for focusing on the interests of only one agent in the dilemma. All affected parties must be given equal consideration. Sure speculative consequences (in this case the likelihood that killings of innocent people will be actually averted) weigh less than certain consequences (the pain inflicted on the suspect), but at some point the speculative side of the scales (where, for example, there are a large number of lives at stake) are so heavy that they outweigh certain bad consequences.

The critics fail to extend their moral horizons beyond the interests of the suspect. This individualistic account of morality represents a far greater threat to our "humanity" than torturing suspects to save lives. A society that stood by and refused to take all reasonable steps to save innocent life would be vastly different to the one in which we currently live. Rescuers would not be permitted to push aside bystanders for fear of bruising them, ambulances would not rush to save sick people for fear of colliding into other cars, police would not pursue criminals for the same reason, people would not undergo security checks at airports before they boarded their planes (because it interfered with their right to liberty and privacy), and we would be content with stating what a pity it is that many innocent were murdered in a possibly preventable incident on the basis that we did not want to apply physical pressure to a suspect. This is approaching moral nihilism.

TORTURE WILL NOT DEHUMANIZE THE TORTURER

A related objection that has been raised to life-saving torture is that it will dehumanize the torturer (as opposed to society in general). The evidence, however, is to the contrary. Throughout history people have been inflicting pain on individuals and sustained no demonstrable moral bruises. Nowadays surgeons do it as part of their day-to-day affairs. While in most countries anesthetic removes the pain during surgery, some forms of surgery cause significant pain and discomfort during the recuperation phase. Moreover, prior to the discovery of anesthetic, surgeons would perform procedures that caused almost unthinkable levels of pain, such as limb amputations.[2] While the goal of the surgeon's action is not to inflict pain, the same applies in relation to the torturer—who is ultimately seeking to save life. Nowadays prison guards lock up prisoners in small cells; some parents still smack their children, and some people kill in self-defense.

Some critics give examples of torturers who have regretted their actions once they have come to learn that their "cause" (for example, warring against another country) was unjust.[3] This is irrelevant to our proposal. We leave no scope for issues of moral subjectivism or relativism or for changed perceptions regarding the justness of torture. Killing innocent people is bad —nearly always so—irrespective of which ideological or normative position one happens to adopt. Proportionate actions taken to prevent this are objectively morally sound[4] and hence (rationally) there is no scope for regret about such matters.

CONCLUSION REGARDING DEHUMANIZING CRITICISM

The dehumanizing criticism is misguided to the point of being contradictory. If standing idly by allowing innocent people to be killed does not dehumanize society, inflicting physical persuasion on a suspect logically cannot. Moreover, all nations permit individuals and security officials to inflict far higher levels of harm, such as killing in self-defense, than torture.[5] If we are not dehumanized now, torture will not make any difference.

CHAPTER SIX

Torture Is Effective

OVERVIEW OF ARGUMENT THAT TORTURE CANNOT WORK AND RESPONSE

The argument that we should not use torture in any circumstances because suspects will not provide the relevant information is potentially a knock-down argument against our proposal. Certainly if this objection was valid we would change our minds and not countenance torture in any circumstances. However, the first thing to note about this argument is that it is not in principle an objection. Rather, it demonstrates a supposed practical flaw identified with life-saving torture. Presumably, if this obstacle was overcome the critics would then agree with the proposal.

The criticism that torture does not work has been advanced by many. The most persuasive paper on the issue is that written by Philip N. S. Rumney.[1] The paper is well measured in its analysis and well researched in its scope. Rumney concludes that torture suspects often do not divulge the information that is sought from them.

There are however two fundamental flaws in his paper in the context of the discussion at hand. None of the instances of torture he considers are similar to the circumstances in which we advocate torture should occur and the means in which it should be administered. Nearly all of the torture cases discussed by the critics involve torture being used for reasons of punishment or domination and humiliation where there is little evidence to suggest that the victim actually possesses the relevant information. Moreover, the pain inflicted was often crude, rather than being inflicted in a clinical institutional setting where the means used are designed to cause the minimum necessary short-term pain while having the least possible long-term effects.

Secondly, the examples Rumney refers to, as wide-ranging as they are, are no more than anecdotal accounts—it is easy to give as many contrary examples where torture was effective.

In relation to many of the examples of torture provided by the critics, torture likely did not work because the victim did not actually have the relevant information (and as a result was forced to lie); other times it would not have had the desired outcome because unsophisticated pain-inducing means were invoked. This is not what is being countenanced by our proposal. Fishing expeditions are not permitted—it must be virtually certain that the suspect has the information.

EXAMPLES OF EFFECTIVE TORTURE

Despite the crude nature of previous incidences of torture, there is a strong evidence that sometimes torture is effective at eliciting information and it does save innocent lives.[2] This is a point accepted by most of the critics.[3] For example, Israeli authorities claim to have foiled ninety terrorist attacks by using coercive interrogation.[4] It is also claimed that information provided as a result of torture enabled the French to foil terrorist attacks in the Algiers.[5] One of the people doing the torturing in the Algiers was General Paul Aussaresses. In his book he cites "a string of instances in which he was able to find bombs and break up terrorist cells as a result of torture." He claims that he quickly discovered that "the best way to make a terrorist talk when they refused to say what he knew was to torture them."[6]

A Bush aide recently noted that torture is an essential tool:

"We're talking about the most successful intelligence gained in the war on terror coming from these programs," he says. Details are hard to come by, but Sen. Kit Bond, a member of the Senate Intelligence Committee, [said] . . . that "enhanced interrogation techniques" worked with at least one high-level Qaeda operative, 9/11 mastermind Khalid Shaikh Mohammed, to thwart a plot. Bond would not say which one, but among foiled plots vaguely described by the White House and linked to "KSM" was a scheme to attack targets on the West Coast of the United States with hijacked airlines. The planning for such a "second wave" attack may have been in the early stages.[7]

A U.S. investigator (by the pseudonym of Chris Mackey) who went to Afghanistan to question Al Qaeda suspects following the U.S. invasion in 2001 has commented that effective interrogation is not possible without the use of torture.[8]

Palmer also notes that in 1995 the Philippines' intelligence service provide information obtained through torture to America that helped foil an Al Qaeda plan to crash eleven planes carrying 4,000 people into the ocean and to crash an explosive-filled Cessna into CIA headquarters.[9] Marcy Strauss gives the example of notorious terrorist Abu Nidel who was "broken" by Jordan officials and the 1993 World Trade Center bombings which were cracked by the Philippines when they threatened to torture a suspect.[10]

Much has been made by the critics of CIA manuals (the *Kubark Counterintelligence Manual* and the *Human Resource Exploitation Manual*) that in parts indicate that torture is often ineffective. It is foolhardy, however, to believe that these documents, which are dated 1963 and 1983, respectively, encompass the sum experiences or collective attitudes of even the CIA toward torture.

If the considered view of the CIA was that torture was not effective in most cases, it seems incredulous that U.S. President George W. Bush and Vice President Dick Cheney would have lobbied Congress so hard to exempt the CIA from legislation (sponsored by Senator John McCain) that bans "cruel, inhuman, and degrading treatment of prisoners in the detention of the U.S. Government" and allow the CIA to torture suspects where this was necessary to prevent a terrorist attack.[11]

Bush initially refused to endorse the Bill, stating that he hoped to reach an agreement with McCain. The agreement being sought related to a proposed narrower definition of torture, which would probably allow some form of harm to be inflicted on wrongdoers.[12] Ultimately, the Bush administration buckled under congressional pressure because repeated prisoner-abuse scandals were proving to be too damaging to America's international reputation. However, this was not until some important concessions were introduced into the Bill, including a defense for people who violated the prohibition in circumstances where they believed they were following a legal order.[13]

After the Bill was passed Senator John McCain conceded that it might not apply in the extremely rare case of a suspect who knew of an imminent attack. In the Bill, torture and cruel, inhumane treatment is defined as that which "shocks the conscience." McCain stated that torture in the ticking time situation, "would not shock the conscience. And in that million-to-one situation, then the president of the United States would authorize it and take responsibility for it."[14]

During this debate, a former top adviser to Bush in Iraq, Robert Blackwill, who was national security adviser during Bush's first term, said that torture should never be totally ruled out. He stated:

> Of course torture should not be widespread and of course there should be extraordinarily stringent top-down requirements in this respect. But never? . . . I wouldn't say never. [Blackwill, answering questions from the audience, said that when he taught a class for executives at Harvard University's John F. Kennedy School of Government, the case that caused the most "confusion" involved a fictional detainee whose organization was threatening to detonate a nuclear weapon in New York City].

You have reason to believe he knows where it is. Do
you torture him? . . . It does seem to me that circumstances matter here and . . . I'm not an absolutist in
this regard.[15]

Recently, U.S. Secretary of State Condoleezza Rice has
claimed that rendition has "prevented attacks in Europe" and
"saved innocent lives."[16] Former President Clinton in October
2006 also stated that in extreme cases the president should be
able to sanction the use of torture.[17] In late September 2006, the
U.S. House of Representatives by a vote of 253 to 168 approved
of the Military Commissions Act (HR6166). The following day
the Senate approved its version of the Bill (S.3930) by a margin
of 65 to 34. The President signed the law on October 17, 2006.
The Act, while ostensibly prohibiting torture was seen as a
major victory for the Bush Administration's tough stance on the
"war on terrorism." The law prohibits "grave breaches" of
Article 3 of the Geneva Convention, including "cruel or inhumane" punishment. The definition of cruel or inhumane in the
bill is so broad that it does not include certain forms of harsh
treatment. Moreover, the President is given the power to inter-
pret the meaning of the Geneva Convention Standards, making
the prohibitions against torture largely discretionary.

Thus, torture is effective sometimes—possibly often. Critics' examples of failed torture can be rebutted by giving at least
an equal number of examples where it has been effective and
further rebutted by the realization that the torture events they
refer to were often punitive fishing exercises—certainly there is
no evidence to suggest that the torturers were overly concerned
to validate that the suspect had the requisite information before
they commenced the torture.

ANECDOTAL EVIDENCE NOT PERSUASIVE

The underlying problem with the way that this aspect of the
debate has developed is that it is in danger of degenerating into

a distracting and superficial numbers game—with the winner supposedly being the side that can provide the most number of examples to support its contention. As is discussed below, the above examples of effective torture are not catalogued to claim victory on this issue, but rather to illustrate how easily the numbers game can be played.

Before moving to more sagacious matters, we underline the futility of the numbers process engaged in by some of the critics. This is a device that has not been confined to the ultimate effectiveness of torture. Some critics have also gone to lengths to discuss the reasons why torture is supposedly unlikely to work. This has even been in relation to issues where the numbers avalanche against them.

Some critics have argued that our proposal is unsound because of the difficulties involved in identifying persons who have the relevant knowledge. To buttress their argument they give examples of errors made by police and security officials in making false arrests.[18] The fallacy in this argument is that it attempts to extrapolate the exception into the rule. For every false arrest it would be possible, literally, to give hundreds and perhaps thousands of examples of the "right" person being detained or questioned. Often there is little doubt that a person is involved in a criminal activity. Sometimes they make admissions, other times they are caught on surveillance cameras before the attack (as were the London bombers in July 2005—although the tape was not noticed until after the bombs exploded), and so on. The fact that sometimes mistakes regarding identity are made is no more an argument against our proposal than it is for abolishing the whole criminal justice system given the number of innocent people that are falsely imprisoned.

Given the clandestine nature of torture and the almost total dearth of reliable data kept, it is verging on intellectual dishonesty to purport to provide an overarching account or precise summary of the extent to which torture victims "fess up."[19] The only salient points to be drawn about the effectiveness of torture are (i) that we know as a fact that humans dislike pain and will try to avoid it, and (ii) all the information from past instances of torture reveals only the following: sometimes it has resulted in suspects divulging information to security officials who have used the information to save other people; sometimes it has not been effective.

It is not easy to find situations where torturers take at least some steps to ensure that the suspect has the relevant knowledge and the torture is not partially at least motivated by an instutionalized dislike of the victim, as is normally the case in relation to war-time situations. Yet it is possible to obtain data that has some usefulness regarding the effectiveness of torture.

In this regard we need to look to more "mundane" instances of torture, as opposed to torture in war-like settings, which is often motivated by intense hatred toward the victim (as opposed to a genuine desire to obtain information—especially information that it is known is in the possession of the victim) and in circumstances where the rule of law is often suspended.

The closest analogy that can be made with our proposal relates to garden-variety police investigations. Police do not normally have a strong desire to punish any particular section of the community and take some steps to ensure that they only arrest people in relation to whom there is evidence of involvement in the crime in question. Sometimes police break the law and beat up suspects in a bid to ascertain the truth. Given that they do not normally have a preexisting dislike of the suspect, their techniques are presumably motivated at least partly by considerations of information gathering so that the crime can be solved. The ultimate motivation, one assumes, is to enhance community safety as opposed to a desire to humiliate or punish the suspect.

In this setting there is a plethora of instances where the will of suspects has been overborne (at least according to the findings of courts) as a result of police beatings, threats, and other acts of thuggery. We are not talking about contrived confessions to stop the beatings and the like, but reliable confessions made to stop the pain.[20]

And if suspects are willing to betray themselves by confessing to crimes which will result in their long-term incarceration, it follows that they will betray their cause and provide information that will save innocent lives.

Moreover, one of the central pillars of the court process in the common law system of justice is built on the bedrock assumption that coercive interrogation works. All people in common law countries must give evidence in court when subpoenaed to do so (save rare exceptions such as legal professional privilege). This is even when they have no connection to the case, apart from having been unfortunate enough to be a witness to a relevant event. Many people have no desire to get involved in any form of litigation. It is often stressful and nearly always time consuming. Sometimes it puts them at risk of reprisal by a party to the proceeding. Despite this, they are always forced to give evidence under threat of imprisonment if they do not. It is assumed that this coerced evidence is truthful. Why should the presumption be displaced when the coercion comes not from the threat of imprisonment but the more acute threat of physical pain?

Thus, the argument that torture never works is unsupportable. Rather, the most accurate assessment of the efficacy of torture as an information-gathering device is that it will sometimes fail, while on other occasions it will succeed. We agree with Rumney that the issue of effectiveness is central in this debate. The way forward here is to obtain more pointed data regarding the circumstances in which torture has been effective and when it has failed. The study could only be retrospective—no one would seriously contemplate actually torturing people for experimental purposes.

The surveyed cases should be confined to instances of torture that as closely as possible resemble the torture framework we suggest, where the mistreatment is not for punitive reasons and the suspect is known to have the relevant information. To this end, the only viable respondents would consist of former and serving police officers, who would need to given a blanket immunity from prosecution for the information that they disclosed.

It is important to note that the results of such a study cannot lead to the conclusion that torture is never justifiable. If it transpires that even the most effective torture techniques only elicit the relevant information in a small number of cases this would mean that the plus side of the scales would need to be heavier than first proposed for torture to be justified. If thousands of lives were at stake even a 20 percent likelihood that torture would be effective would justify its use.

Ultimately, we cannot be guaranteed that torture will work in any given instance, but we can be virtually certain that doing nothing will fail when we are faced with an imminent catastrophe.

CONCLUSION REGARDING ARGUMENT THAT TORTURE IS NOT EFFECTIVE

There is no relevant evidence that torture cannot work in the circumstances we outline. The "evidence" to the contrary that is proffered by the critics has been overstated in terms of its relevance to our proposal. The empirical data cited by the critics regarding the outcome of other incidents of torture can be dismissed on the basis that it occurred in a different setting to that we propose. Reported incidents of torture are invariably crude acts of violence done for reasons of punishment, domination, and humiliation in circumstances where there is little basis for believing that the victim has relevant information. This is qualitatively different to inflicting physical persuasion in a clinical setting where the suspect is known to have the relevant information. Having said that, even in relation to the crude forms of torture that have been practiced the evidence shows that this has been effective in saving many lives.

Related to this point is the argument that we should never torture because we can never be sure that the suspect has the relevant information. This is wrong. We can be sure of this, at least to the same degree of certainty that is required before we take other decisive steps, such as acting in self-defense or imprisoning or executing prisoners or going to war against other countries. Like all decisions, we must base our choices on the best evidence at the time. A requirement of perfect knowledge as a precondition to action would freeze all human activity—we would not even go to work in the morning because we could never be sure that we would not be hit by the next bus. There is no logical basis for demanding perfect knowledge only in proposed cases of torture. The fact that this argument has no credibility in other contexts shows that it is a misapprehension in the context of torture.

CHAPTER SEVEN

Torture Is Not Antidemocratic

MOST PEOPLE FAVOR TORTURE

Another supposed downside of torture is that it is antidemocratic or will corrupt democracy. Some critics have even put it as high as that it will have a "devastating effect" on democracy.[1] This is a confusing argument because its main premise is not spelled out. Democracy is a complex and ill-defined notion. If it means majoritarianism, as many believe to be the case, then a lawfully elected government can obviously through its normal political process legalize torture. If the normal law-making process is observed, then life-saving torture and democracy sit harmoniously.

It is certainly not inconceivable that a robust and free democracy would permit life-saving torture. The latest *Newsweek* poll on the subject shows that:

> 44 percent of the public thinks torture is often or sometimes justified as a way to obtain important information, while 51 percent say it is rarely or never justified. A clear majority—58 percent—would support torture to thwart a terrorist attack, but asked if they would still support torture if that made it more likely enemies would use it against Americans, 57 percent

said no. Some 73 percent agree that America's image abroad has been hurt by the torture allegations.[2]

These findings are confirmed by a more wide-ranging poll by AP-Ipsos reported in December 2005. It showed that in addition to Americans, a majority of people in Britain, France, and South Korea also approved of torturing terrorism suspects in rare instances. In Canada, Mexico, and Germany, the community is split on whether torture is justified in any circumstances. Of the nine countries surveyed, only majorities in Spain and Italy opposed torture in all circumstances.[3]

SOCIETIES, WHEN PRESSED, ALWAYS CHOOSE THE LESSER EVIL

Moreover, as we noted in chapter 2, when (democratic) societies have their backs to the wall and they are forced to make difficult choices, they invariably go down the path of least harm. In chapter 3, we gave several examples of the preparedness of governments to sacrifice the interests of individuals for the greater good, such as forcing soldiers to go to war and the like. The principle behind such decisions has not been challenged by the critics. But for illustrative purposes we add to the catalogue of situations that make it clear that, when forced to chose between two evils, we always elect for the lesser evil. Notions of individual rights go missing in the process.

The English Court of Appeal in the case of *Re A (Children)* in 2000 held that it was permissible to kill one conjoined twin in order to improve the chances that the other would live. This was despite the fact that there was no guarantee that the stronger twin would survive the operation.[4] Why did the Court make this decision? Pressed to make a choice between important conflicting rights, the judge resolved the matter "by choosing the lesser of the two evils and so finding the least detrimental alternative."[5]

For another "real life" example of what we do in extreme cases, refer to the Zeebrugge disaster in 1987. Dozens of people were in the water and in danger of drowning. They were near the foot of a rope ladder, but their route to safety was blocked for at least ten minutes by a young man who was petrified by cold or fear (or both) and was unable to move. The corporeal gave instructions to push him off the ladder. He was never seen again. What if instead of blocking the ladder the young man refused to provide the pin number to release the ladder? There is not too much doubt that he would have been subjected to some "physical persuasion."

Continuing with the real-life theme (to finally bury the claim that the examples we cite belong in the realms of fiction), as noted in the previous chapter, most countries have laws that compel witnesses to give evidence in court. This is even if they do not wish to and in fact have strong reasons for not giving evidence. Yet we compel them to do so, no matter what level of mental anguish this causes them and the level of danger that this places them in. A recent illustration involves twenty-seven-year-old Melbourne lawyer Zarah Garde-Williams. She was found guilty of contempt of court for refusing to testify against two "gangsters" who had murdered her boyfriend. The murders were in the context of unprecedented underworld killings in Melbourne resulting in the execution-style killings of more than 20 "gangland" figures over several years. During questions by the judge about her involvement with the victim (her former boyfriend), she wept in the witness box and responded that she was "unable to answer questions due to fear for [her] safety." One of the accused threatened her and she said that she believed she would get her "head blown off" if she gave evidence. She applied to enter a police witness protection program but this was rejected. Still, the fact that Ms. Garde-Williams thought she would be killed if she gave evidence and was obviously traumatized about the prospect of giving evidence did not find much favor with the judge. In finding her guilty of contempt for refusing to answer the questions, Justice Harper stated that her fear was no excuse for not giving evidence and that if other witnesses in murder trials also refused to testify, "no system of justice could survive."[6]

Thus, here we have a situation where the criminal justice system is using the threat of imprisonment to coerce information from a traumatized innocent individual who has reasonable grounds for believing that she would be killed if she obeyed the law. Given a choice between this ordeal and a dose of physical persuasion there would be no doubt that many people would prefer the former. As a community we often treat individuals very harshly when the common good is at stake. It is an undeniable fact. Yet democracy remains in tact.

And as a side issue, note the absence of the arguments that are used against our life-saving torture proposal in the context of compelled witness disclosure. In this context, there are no utterances along the lines that we should not force witnesses to give evidence because we can never be sure that the witness has the evidence, the witness might lie, and so on. These arguments resonate very strongly with the torture critics but are muted in the context of other institutionalized practices that can have a crushing impact on individuals. These arguments are in reality just as futile in the context of torture.

Some critics have sought to pad out the notion of democracy slightly by suggesting that it is built on the foundation of respect for individuals and human rights and that torture runs counter to this. This in essence is the dehumanizing point repeated under a different banner. If democracy does entail respect for individuals and human rights, then surely each individual counts equally in this process, including that of potential victims.

Even if we move from strictly majoritarianism accounts of democracy to more expansive and sophisticated accounts of the nature of democracy, which contend that democracy is a substantive rather than a procedural concept, there seems no scope for labelling the institutionalization of life-saving torture as a threat to democracy. For example, the democratic ideal adopted by Samuel Freeman provides that the only political and social institutions that are justifiable by Democratic sovereignty are those that reflect the interests common to all people. It can hardly be doubted that the highest-order interest shared by at least most people is the right to life.[7]

Moreover, as is noted by Palmer, countries such as France, Britain, and Israel have all used torture widely over the past fifty years and "none has sunk into barbarism, or ceased to be a law-governed democracy."[8]

If the critics want to persuasively advance the democracy counter, they need to spell out the key indicia of such a concept and how it is incompatible with going down the path of the lesser evil. The critics have much work to do on this front.

CONCLUSION REGARDING ANTIDEMOCRATIC ARGUMENT

The antidemocratic criticism is factually wrong. The history of humankind shows that when societies are threatened they prioritize the common good over individual interests. This was a point developed in chapter 3. The critics have not referred to a single counterexample to our claim.

CHAPTER EIGHT

The Real Divide

Where Responsibility Starts and Ends

WHY THERE IS NO AGREEMENT ON TORTURE

Despite the size of the apparent gulf between us and the critics, in important respects there is considerable consensus. We both approach the issue from the perspective that it is bad to inflict pain, and we agree that compassion should drive moral outcomes. While there is disagreement regarding the effectiveness of torture, this relates to a difference in degree, not nature (the critics do not contend that torture never works). And we are confident that the critics would agree the right to life is more important that the right to physical integrity—at least we doubt that a tenable argument could be mounted to the contrary.

Thus, the main central point of difference that remains is the application of the slippery slope argument. This does not seem to appear to be sufficient to explain the gulf between our respective views.

THE NOTION OF PERSONAL RESPONSIBILITY

In our view, a large part of the reason for the difference in our conclusions on torture relates to a notion that has not featured

in the surface nature of the debate. This is the notion of responsibility. The fundamental divide between us and the critics is
that invariably when they present their views they focus on the
brutality of torture. On the other hand, we focus on the need to
save innocent lives. The critics rarely comment on the other side
of their antitorture proposal—the cruelty associated with standing idly by as innocent people are killed. This point is also made
by Louis Seidman:

> [Opponents of torture] focus on the human suffering
> imposed by the use of certain techniques but are
> unwilling to broaden their concern to suffering that
> might be caused by the failure to use them. Instead,
> many of them adopt as an article of faith that these
> techniques are never useful.[1]

The moral horizons of the critics, it seems, are transfixed
on the plight of the suspect. This is arbitrary. The critics need to
lift their horizons and consider the interests of all the parties
whose interests are likely to be affected by the decision regarding whether or not to torture the suspect. This is a glaring fail-
ure on behalf of the critics. Thus, we are not told, for example,
what response is suitable to give to the relatives of innocent
people killed in a potentially preventable murderous act. A copy
of the Convention against Torture, even if framed, would surely
not suffice.

This involves some speculation, but the reason that the critics do not go *there*—and spell out which principle justifies not
acting to save the innocent people—we believe is because they
are (indirectly) relying on what is potentially the strongest counterargument to the proposal to allow life-saving torture.

A criticism that is often made of utilitarianism is that it
does not give sufficient space for people to pursue their individual projects and requires us to take too much responsibility for actions and events not of our doing. The classic
illustration of this is the famous Jim and Pedro example by
Bernard Williams.

Jim is a botanist on an expedition in a small South American town where the ruthless government regards him as an honored visitor from another land. He goes into town and sees twenty Indians tied up. Pedro, the captain in charge, explains that the Indians are a random group of inhabitants who, after recent protests against the government, are about to be executed to deter others from protesting. Since Jim is an honored guest, Pedro offers him the "privilege" of killing one of the Indians himself. If he accepts, as a special mark of the occasion, the other Indians will be spared. If he refuses, they will all be killed. Jim realizes it is impossible to take the guns and kill Pedro and the large number of other soldiers. The Indians and other soldiers understand the situation, and the Indians are begging for him to take up the offer.[2]

Williams argues that if Jim were a utilitarian he would kill the Indian. Williams himself has trouble accepting this outcome. Williams' quarrel is not necessarily with the result that utilitarianism commits one to (in fact, he has subsequently stated that he too would shoot the Indian), but with the reasoning process employed by the utilitarian to resolve the dilemma. Williams contends that utilitarianism cuts out considerations that most would think integral to such cases, such as the idea that each of us is specially responsible for what we do, rather than what others do. This, therefore, supposedly makes utilitarianism unintelligible, because it fails to appreciate the relationship between a man and his projects.

Antitorture proponents, at least implicitly, by failing to expressly consider the interests of the innocent people at risk, seem to be endorsing this account of personal responsibility. There is some merit in this view. As individuals, we cannot be expected to take responsibility and attempt to correct all the potential injustices that we can potentially cure. This would make life intolerable and cut us off from many of the activities that give life meaning and purpose. People achieve happiness not only by making other people happy but through a vast range of projects such as being committed to persons, causes, institutions, or a range of other activities.[3]

WE ARE RESPONSIBLE FOR FAILING
TO SAVE INNOCENT PEOPLE

However, the notion of personal responsibility is ultimately not so narrow as to enable societies to avoid responsibility for preventable deaths. At the personal level, our obligations are circumscribed by the maxim of positive duty. This is the view that we must assist others in serious trouble, *when assistance would immensely help them at no or little inconvenience to ourselves.*[4]

There are occasions when acting morally requires us to do more than merely refraining from certain behavior; where we must actually *do* something. Morality defined exhaustively as a set of negative proscriptions fails to explain why it is morally repugnant for Bill Gates to refuse to give his loose change to the starving peasant whose path he crosses, or why it is wrong to decline to save the child drowning in a puddle in order to avoid getting our shoes wet, or to refuse to throw a life rope to the person drowning beside the pier.

Torturing a suspect to save other people from being killed arguably does not come within this principle—inflicting pain on another person is no minor inconvenience.

However, different considerations apply regarding governmental obligations and the institutionalization of practices. Governments have a duty to put in place practices and processes that balance the countervailing interests of all the citizenry regarding the actual and foreseeable practices and events. Thus, they are required to form defense forces, police forces, courts, and hospitals. In the operation of such institutions, each individual's interests must count equally.

Given that it is foreseeable that people will continue to engage in activities that threaten the lives of others, it is remiss of the government not to develop a framework for dealing with such scenarios. The number of situations where such a framework may be used will be rare, but given the enormity of issues at hand the matter cannot be ignored.

Thus, the critics have no basis for considering only one aspect of the torture equation when they are developing their responses. If torture is never permissible, they are required to explain which account of responsibility shields them from being responsible for the deaths of innocent people whom they refused to assist. There is much work on this front, as well.

CHAPTER NINE

Why the Torture Debate *Really* Matters

(And Why A *"Meta-analysis"* of the Torture Debate Supports Our Argument)

THE HARM CAUSED BY ALLEGIANCE
TO RIGHTS THEORIES

Hopefully, we will never find ourselves in a situation where a torture warrant may be issued. Despite the scarcity with which such situations may occur, the torture debate is important. This is because it highlights many of the failings of current moral thinking that are responsible for an enormous amount of preventable suffering in the world. As noted in chapter 3, contemporary moral discourse is dominated by (nonconsequentialist) rights-based theories.

In that chapter we argued that these theories are flawed. They have no foundation and are unable to provide persuasive answers to central issues regarding their justification and provenance. Rights as used in conventional moral discourse are, as Jeremy Bentham taught us about two hundred years ago, "nonsense on stilts."

In the end there is no basis upon which to distinguish real from illusory rights and no way of determining which right wins when there is a clash of rights. Given that rights have no justification, when they clash the winner is often the person who yells the loudest.

Despite the fact that rights are nonsense, we like rights. They appeal to those of us who have a "me, me, me" approach to moral issues. But buried only slightly beneath such an approach are the inescapable realities that as people we live in communities; communities are merely the sum of a number of other individuals; and the actions of one person (exercising his or her rights) can have an (negative) effect on the interests of others. While rights seek to "atomize" people, the reality of the human condition is that we don't and can't function (happily) without the involvement of others.[1]

The two principal problems associated with endorsing a moral code that approaches moral dilemmas through the prism of rights is that the moral horizon is limited to oneself and those directly within one's view and there is no mechanism for ranking rights. This makes it very easy (if not encourages) for us to be preoccupied with our interests and place our minor concerns above life and death concerns of other (especially distant) people. Rights are good devices for deflecting moral responsibility.

As a result, human rights discourse is effective only at the conversational level. The promises of grandiose international and national rights-based documents have bypassed a large portion of the world's population. Many people are not even capable of reading the documents or are too hungry or too hot or too cold to summon the energy to inquire what they contain. Thus, while the surface nature of our language and discourse almost unquestionably accepts the existence of human rights—and "universal" ones at that—there is a huge gap between our acts and words when it comes to rights.[2] We are good at talking up rights and even asserting *our* rights but deficient when it comes to securing the rights of others—especially the people we are not directly confronted with.

"There is enough grain alone produced to provide every human being on the planet with 3,500 calories a day—enough to make most people fat."[3] Yet more than 13,000 people are starving daily while much of the Western World is gorging itself to ill health on super-sized meals.[4] How can this situation occur?

A significant part of the answer rests in the fact that we "operate" in a moral framework that is individualizing, has no express regard for the common good, and provides no clear guidance regarding the interests that matter most to human flourishing. One of us has previously argued that in order to eradicate the gross inequities in the world we must debunk a number of existing normative and psychological fallacies from our collective psyches. This includes a belief in baseless forms of rights.

THE FAILINGS OF OUR MORAL CODE ILLUSTRATED BY THE BAN ON TORTURE

The subject of torture provides an excellent illustration of much of what is wrong with prevailing rights orthodoxy. It highlights:

(i) The horizon-limiting affect of such theories. As noted above, the critics do not address the rights of the innocent people whose lives are at risk, instead confining their gaze to the person immediately before them (the suspect);

(ii) The absence of a mechanism for ranking rights and the problems associated with a belief in absolute rights. Thus, we see that the critics are committed to the untenable position that the right to life is lower down the rights hierarchy than the right to physical integrity.

(iii) The fact that (given the formless nature of contemporary rights-based theories) moral debates are often dominated not by reasoned arguments but emotive utterances—without any degree of apparent incoherency or impertinence—thereby stifling moral progress.

The third point is aptly illustrated by the manner in which this debate has been played out, particularly in the Australian context, where passion clearly trumped clear thinking.[5]

THE DANGER OF LETTING EMOTION TRUMP LOGIC

This "chest-thumping" and disparaging approach to moral discourse was not confined to the utterances of lay people, who may have understandably been jarred by the proposal to allow torture in, albeit, limited circumstances.

Thus, we see that in the paper by O'Rourke et al. in the *University of San Francisco Law Review*, we are referred to as "apologists" for torture—several times, just in case the point was missed the first time. This is despite the fact that, as we noted previously, our theory would justify very few instances of torture. We are no more apologists for torture than O'Rourke et al. are apologists for murder (of the lives they are unprepared to try to save). We have little doubt that this point was not missed on them, but it is only in the context of a moral code whose contours are so formless that this type of approach would be regarded as being credible.

The president of an organization called Liberty Victoria (which is thanked by O'Rourke et al. in their paper for providing helpful comments) stated that the article in which we proposed life-saving torture was a "stain" on the reputation of our law school (apparently the concepts of free speech and prohibition of guilt by association do not rank highly on that organization's ideals). The Immigration Lawyers Association of Australasia stated that our views were "offensive, unforgivable, and even barbaric." Letters were sent to editors of the *University of San Francisco Law Review* (where our first paper on torture was published) urging it to not publish the paper, and some law groups and even politicians called for one of us to be sacked from a position as a member of the Refugee Review Tribunal,[6] and so on.

This type of discourse by seemingly intelligent and well-intentioned people could only occur in the context of a discipline that is bereft of an intellectual framework. To this end, the most telling aspect of this debate is that none of the critics have attempted to develop an alternative moral framework to the consequentialist ethic that we endorse. O'Rourke et al. refer to our underlying theory as a "feeble consequentialist ethic," apparently with little regard to the fact that utilitarianism has been the main driver of political and social development for at least two centuries, until the past several decades.

Certainly, it is appropriate to criticize utilitarianism, but to do so effectively requires *reasons* in support of such a contention. The remark that it must be wrong because it leads to bad outcomes was dealt with in chapter 3—as a society, when we find ourselves in a jam we do (and should) follow the path of harm minimization—this is the ultimate "tie breaker." To persuasively criticize our account requires the advancement of an alternative moral theory that can provide coherent answers across the whole spectrum of moral issues that we as individuals and together as a society face from time to time.

Absent such a theory we get randomness, or worse still, the domination of those prone to high emotion with loud voices—the antithesis of a moral code.

To illustrate this point, we provide two examples of the problems that beset theorists who do not endorse a utilitarian approach. They come from responses to our paper published in the *Deakin Law Review*. The first is a paper by John Kleinig, who elegantly advances many of the criticisms that we rebut in this book. Ostensibly, many readers will be attracted to some of his arguments, but his approach collapses when he actually addresses the proposal at hand. At a lecture on torture delivered several days after the opinion piece was published in *The Age*, he said that our proposal was illogical.

> The Deakin lecturers' argument—that torture in extreme situations may be justified because the interests of many can outweigh the suffering of a few—was inhumane and illogical.[7]

However, he then conceded that "if Melbourne were under threat of a nuclear attack, which was then averted by torturing a confession from a suspect, he [Kleinig] would be relieved."

His resolution of this apparent contradiction:

> That may be the one situation where we as a society might say, "You went out on a limb and did something

we're totally opposed to, but it had a good result, so we forgive you."

This is the sort of confusion that occurs if moral dilemmas are approached on the basis of piecemeal solutions without the support of underlying theories. When nonconsequentialist theories are applied to hard cases (instead of avoiding them), they become unstable, often leading to unprincipled compromises. This is because they are lacking in substance, meaning that their proponents are reduced to relying on "fine phrases . . . the last resort of those who have run out of arguments."[8]

This is highlighted by the contribution of Desmond Manderson to the debate. He offers an impassioned argument against torture. In the end, his reasons for dismissing life-saving torture are:

moral

> Torture is wrong under all circumstances, not because it leads to certain bad outcomes, but for no reason: simply and inherently. This is not a perverse argument. Love, for example, is good not because it might lead us to wealth or happiness, but for no reason. It just is. In fact, to look for reasons, to ask "what is love good for" or "how does loving someone benefit me"? is a sign of psychopathy. If Bagaric and Faris and Clarke cannot see the inherent wrong of torture, it is hard to see how to communicate with them.[9]

In fact, moral discourse does require reasons, otherwise yelling wins the day. The emptiness of Manderson's "reasoning" is highlighted by substituting "women's rights" for "torture" in the above quote and studying the evolution of the women's movement in the United States as recently as 150 years ago or in contemporary Iran or Saudi Arabia. Moreover, love is not self-evidently good—hence the reason for so many domestic killings in the "name of love." In the end, only consequences matter.

The manner in which this debate has been played out in fact provides a good example of the distortions in moral belief and social commentary that can occur in a moral vacuum. Perhaps in the end, moral judgments are simply emotive retorts that are dressed up in a veneer of objectivity in order that they can be used as argumentative levers to attempt to shape the behavior of others. The once-popular meta-ethical theory of emotivism suggested this. However, in our view it is premature to give up searching for universal moral standards. This can only be frustrated by providing a receptive ear to emotional retorts, no matter how loudly or frequently they are expressed.

The problems with rights-based theories provide compelling reasons, as illustrated by consideration of the subject of torture, for endorsing the moral theory that we advanced in chapter 3: utilitarianism. In this context there is a clear framework for settling moral disputes. The proposal that wins is that which will best enhance human flourishing, where each person's interest counts equally (whether they are a suspect or potential victim and irrespective of where in the world they have the fortune or misfortune of being born).

TORTURE IS ALREADY LAWFUL

Perhaps the most surprising aspect of the emotion generated by our torture paper (and why we are relatively confident that the critics lost perspective of the wider issues at hand and were swept away by the pejorative connotation attached to the word "torture") is that if our proposal to allow warrants to be issued in life-saving circumstances was adopted it would probably narrow the circumstances in which torture is currently lawful.

The common law defense of necessity (which has at its base the same utilitarian foundation as self-defense) has three requirements:

(i) The act [the infliction of physical pain] is needed to avoid inevitable and irreparable evil [the death of innocent people];

(ii) No more should be done than is reasonably necessary for the purpose to be achieved; and

(iii) The evil inflicted must not be disproportionate to the evil avoided.

In the United States, the defense is typically spelled out in simpler terms, but it has the same key features. Necessity applies where an accused reasonably believed his or her harmful actions were necessary to avert a greater, imminent harm.[10]

Now juxtapose this with the circumstances in which we suggest that torture is permissible. Torture should be permissible where the following conditions are satisfied:

(i) When *innocent lives* (not other, lesser interests) are at risk;

(ii) There is a *near certainty* that the suspect has the relevant information; and

(iii) The pain inflicted is the minimum necessary to elicit the information and aims to have no lasting effects.

Our proposal has the additional safeguard that torture must be approved by a judicial officer *before* it occurs, not leaving it to law enforcement officers to make the judgment and then testing after the event whether they complied with the law.

Our standard is narrower because the only threats that justify torture are to life (not lesser interests), and we require a higher level of confidence that the suspect has the information.[11]

It is also noteworthy that while the law previously held that necessity could not justify killing another person to ward off a greater threat, this no longer seems to be the case, at least in the United Kingdom, following the decision in *Re A (Children)* in 2000. In our home state of Victoria, legislation recently passed removes any doubt that in fact necessity is a defense to killing. The *Crimes (Homicide) Act* introduces a defense of "sudden or extraordinary emergency," exculpating killing where it is reasonable in the circumstances.[12] This could extend to torture. If the victim/suspect does not die, the common law of necessity will continue to apply.

It is astounding that these points were missed in the context of an "informed" debate, especially by lawyers and legal academics. The explanation for this is that the debate has not been informed at all. It is a classic example of emotion trumping clear thinking. The fact that our contemporary moral thinking is so blurred that such arguments still have a veneer of plausibility provides strong reasons for moving to a new moral framework.[13]

CHAPTER 10

Conclusion

The End Justifies the Means

There is yet one criticism of the permissibility of life-saving torture that has not been considered. We leave it to last because it underscores the barrenness of the claims that torture is never justifiable.

Perhaps the most common criticism to our proposal is that the "end does not justify the means." This criticism in fact bites the critics far harder than it does our proposal and highlights a central failing in their approach.

The critics presumably have some end in mind as well. At least we have declared what we believe the ultimate end to be: net human flourishing, where each person's interests count equally. If the end (measured in human flourishing) does not justify the means, what, then, does? At best the critics "end" seems to be that there should be an absolute ban on torture. This, however, is not a principle. It is a narrow rule applying to a specific moral dilemma. Presumably, it is derived from the pursuit of a wider objective. Until this wider objective is revealed there is no basis for believing that the conclusions reached by some of the critics are other than prereflective visceral responses to our proposal. It is far better to have a stated (albeit contentious) end than none at all; otherwise, randomness will continue to be the one constant of our collective moral sentiments.

The torture debate highlights the failings of contemporary moral discourse. The circumstances in which torture is morally permissible will hopefully be rare, but they are foreseeable. If they do arise it is important that we adopt the life-affirming approach. It is obviously bad to inflict physical pain on suspects, but it is much worse to allow innocent people to be murdered. This conclusion is evident from the fact that there is no underlying theory that even purports to justify the view that the right to life is less important than the right to physical integrity.

Critics reject the proposal that life-saving torture is morally permissible principally because they do not extend their moral horizons far enough to consider the interests of the innocent people whose lives are at stake. This, however, is largely not their fault. Nonwillful blindness is a byproduct of the warped and largely formless moral code that transcends much of contemporary Western thinking.

The most important lesson from the torture debate is that the only absolute principle is that there is no absolute principle, and the closest that we get to coming to one is that the ultimate moral standard is that we must act to maximize human flourishing, where each individual's interest counts equally—even those who are not immediately before us.

While the critics have been confused, one hopes that they are not incorrigible and that they finally take a few steps up the moral mountain beyond the rights fog in which they are currently enveloped—it would make the world a far better place.

Notes

1. INTRODUCTION: OVERVIEW OF THE TORTURE DEBATE

1. Israel was the last state to officially sanction the practice. *Use of Torture against Palestinian Political Prisoners* (Feb. 2000), *at* http://www.totse.com/en/politics/the_world_beyond_ the_usa/164142.html) (last accessed Mar. 8, 2005). At least after the Landau Report of 1987, and for some time before, the nature of the conduct sanctioned by Israel was ambiguous, and precise interrogation methods were classified as secret. The Israeli government denied the interrogation methods employed amounted to torture. See, e.g., Statement by Israeli Representative at 18th Session of United Nations Committee against Torture, (May 7, 1997), ISRAEL MINISTRY OF FOREIGN AFFAIRS, at http://www.mfa.gov.il/MFA/Foreign+Relations/Israel+and+the+ UN/Speeches+-+statements/. After the Landau Report of 1987, the Israeli government only admitted to using "moderate physical pressure" and in some cases "enhanced physical pressure" for purposes of interrogation, still claiming that this did not amount to torture. However, in May 1998 the United Nations Committee against Torture found that the interrogation methods used in Israel, of which it was aware, constituted torture. *Conclusions and Recommendations of the Committee against Torture: Israel*, U.N. HCHR, 27th Sess., at 1, U.N. Doc. CAT/C/XXVII/Concl.5 (2001). Nevertheless, the practices continued without judicial intervention until September 1999, when the Israeli Supreme Court ruled it illegal. Steve Weizman, *Israel Uses Torture in Defiance of Court Ban*, INDEP. (London), Nov.

12, 2001, available at http://news.independent.co.uk/world/ middle_east/story.jsp?story=104447. Despite this ruling, it has been suggested that the Israeli authorities continue to use torture. *Id.* Ken Roth, the executive director of Human Rights Watch, suggests that Israel ended up torturing around 90 percent of its Palestinian security detainees until finally the Israeli supreme court outlawed the practice. Interview by Wolf Blitzer with Alan Dershowitz, Professor of Law, Harvard University, and Ken Roth, *Dershowitz: Torture Could Be Justified* (Mar. 3, 2003), *available at* http://edition.cnn.com/2003/LAW/03/03/ cnna.Dershowitz.

2. For example, see Richard J. Wilson, United States Detainees at Guantánamo Bay: The Inter-American Commission on Human Rights Responds to a "Legal Black Hole," 10 HUM. RTS. BRIEF 2 (2004).

3. *Legal Definitions of Torture Not Black and White*, CNN, May 11, 2004, at http://www.cnn.com/2004/LAW/05/10/ torture.legal.ap: "The [U.S.] Defense Department is investigating more than forty cases of possible misconduct against civilians in Iraq and Afghanistan, including as many as twelve unjustified deaths. The CIA inspector general, meantime, is looking into three detainee deaths during or after interrogations with agency personnel."

4. Interview by Wolf Blitzer with Alan Dershowitz, Professor of Law, Harvard University, and Ken Roth, *Dershowitz: Torture Could Be Justified* (Mar. 3, 2003), *available at* http:// edition.cnn.com/2003/LAW/03/03/cnna.Dershowitz.

5. James Silver, *Why America's Top Liberal Lawyer Wants to Legalise Torture*, THE SCOTSMAN, May 22, 2004, available at http://thescotsman.scotsman.com/international. cfm?id=582662004 (quoting Alan Dershowitz). Dershowitz summarizes his stance on torture as follows: "I am generally against torture as a normative matter, and I would like to see its use minimized. I believe that at least moderate forms of nonlethal torture are in fact being used by the United States and some of its allies today. I think that if we ever confronted an

actual case of imminent mass terrorism that could be prevented by the infliction of torture we would use torture (even lethal torture), and the public would favor its use. That is my empirical conclusion. It is either true or false, and time will probably tell." Alan M. Dershowitz, *The Torture Warrant: A Response to Professor Strauss* 48 N.Y.L. SCH. L. REV. 275, 277 (2004).

6. "'Everybody says they're opposed to torture. But everyone would do it personally if they knew it could save the life of a kidnapped child who had only two hours of oxygen left before death. And it would be the right thing to do.'" Vicki Haddock (quoting Alan Dershowitz), *The Unspeakable: To Get the Truth, Is Torture or Coercion Ever Justified?* S.F. CHRON., Nov. 18, 2001, available at http://www.sfgate.com/cgi-bin/article.cgi?file=/chronicle/archive/2001/11/18/IN238544.DTL&type=printable. See also poll results of Americans and people in eight other countries discussed in chapter 7.

7. C L Ten, CRIME, GUILT, AND PUNISHMENT 18–25 (1987).

8. *Id.*

2. TORTURE: REALITY AND LEGAL POSITION

1. Convention against Torture and Other Cruel, Inhuman, or Degrading Treatment or Punishment, G.A. Res. 39/46, U.N. GAOR, Supp. No. 51, at 197, U.N. Doc.A/29/51 (1984), art. 1. This is the definition of torture that we use in this book.

2. Amnesty International has observed that "numerous new international standards have been adopted prohibiting torture and setting out governments' obligations to prevent it. An impressive array of international human rights mechanisms has been put in place to press states to live up to their commitments." AMNESTY INT'L., TORTURE WORLDWIDE: AN AFFRONT TO HUMAN DIGNITY 2 (2000). For an excellent overview of the prohibition against torture, see Conor Foley, COMBATING TORTURE: A MANUAL FOR JUDGES & PROSECUTORS §1.9–1.10, available at www.essex.ac.uk/combatingtorturehandbook/manual   (last

accessed Feb. 13, 2005). Much of the foregoing overview of the law of torture is derived from this source.

3. *General Comment on Issues Relating to Reservations Made upon Ratification or Accession to the Covenant or the Optional Protocols Thereto, or in Relation to Declarations under Article 41 of the Covenant*, U.N. Committee on Human Rights, General Comment 24, at 52, para. 10 U.N. Doc. CCPR/C/21/Rev.1/Add.6 (1994).

4. G.A. Res. 217 A(III), U.N. Doc. A/810 at 71 (1948) [hereinafter UDHR].

5. G.A. Res. 2200A (XXI), U.N. GOAR, 21st Sess., Supp. No. 16, at 52, U.N. Doc. A/6316 (1966) [hereinafter ICCPR].

6. European Convention for the Protection of Human Rights and Fundamental Freedoms, Sep. 3, 1953, 213 U.N.T.S. 222.

7. Nov. 22, 1969, O.A.S. Treaty Series No. 36, at 1, OEA/Ser.L./V/II.23 doc. rev. 2.

8. June 27, 1981, OAU Doc. CAB/LEG/67/3 rev. 5, 21 I.L.M. 58.

9. Strasbourg, 26.XI.1987, E.T.S. 126, entered into force Feb. 1, 1989.

10. Feb. 28, 1987, O.A.S. Treaty Series No. 67, OEA/Ser.L.V/II.82 doc.6 rev.1 at 83.

11. U.N. Convention Against Torture.

12. See Conor Foley, COMBATING TORTURE: A MANUAL FOR JUDGES & PROSECUTORS §1.9–1.10.

13. AMNESTY INT'L., TORTURE WORLDWIDE: AN AFFRONT TO HUMAN DIGNITY 2 (2000), at 10.

14. See, e.g., Geneva Convention for the Amelioration of the Condition of the Wounded and Sick in Armed Forces in the Field, Aug. 12, 1949, arts. 12 & 50, 75 U.N.T.S. 38, 62 [hereinafter Geneva Convention I]; Geneva Convention for the Amelioration of the Condition of the Wounded, Sick, and Shipwrecked Members of Armed Forces at Sea, Aug. 12, 1949, arts. 12 & 51, 75 U.N.T.S 94, 116 [hereinafter Geneva Convention

II]; Geneva Convention Relative to the Treatment of Prisoners of War, Aug. 12, 1949, arts. 13, 14, 87 & 130, 75 U.N.T.S. 146, 148, 202, 238 [hereinafter Geneva Convention III].

15. Thus, Art. 7 of the Rome Statute of the International Criminal Court, U.N. Doc. A/CONF.183/9 (1998), includes torture and rape within the International Criminal Court's jurisdiction.

16. James Silver, *Why America's Top Liberal Lawyer Wants to Legalise Torture*, THE SCOTSMAN, May 22, 2004.

17. AMNESTY INT'L., TORTURE WORLDWIDE: AN AFFRONT TO HUMAN DIGNITY 2 (2000), at 10.

18. *Id.* at 10.

19. Allegro Pacheco, PUBLIC COMMITTEE AGAINST TORTURE IN ISRAEL, PROVING TORTURE: NO LONGER NECESSARY IN ISRAEL (1999), at http://internationalstudies.uchicago.edu/torture/abstracts/allegrapacheo.html.

20. *Id.* Many of these "methods" are alleged to have been used in the interrogation of prisoners by United States military personal in Abu Ghraib prison, Iraq. See Scott Higham and Joe Stephens, *Secret Detainee Statements Reveal Savagery of Abu Ghraib*, THE AGE (Australia), May 22, 2004, at 17; Seymour M. Hersh, *Torture at Abu Ghraib*, THE NEW YORKER, May 10, 2004, at 42.

21. James Silver, *Why America's Top Liberal Lawyer Wants to Legalise Torture*.

22. Peter Finn, *Police Torture Threat Sparks Painful Debate in Germany*, WASH. POST, Mar. 8, 2003, at A19.

23. John Hooper, *Germany Racked by Torture Controversy*, THE AGE (Australia), Feb. 28, 2003, at http://theage.com.au/articles/2003/02/27/1046064162443.html.

24. Peter Finn, *Police Torture Threat Sparks Painful Debate in Germany*.

25. *Police Threat Fuels Debate on Torture*, DEUTSCHE WELLE (Germany), Feb. 24, 2003, at http://www.dw-world.de/english/0,3367,1430_A_785751,00.html. The precise nature of

the warning is not clear. The kidnapper has alleged that he was told a specialist was being flown to Frankfurt who could inflict on him "pain of the sort [he] had never before experienced." The police deputy commissioner has denied this account but admitted that it was made very plain to the suspect that they would hurt him until he "identified the whereabouts of the child." Hooper, *supra* note 23. The suspect pleaded guilty at trial, was pronounced guilty of abduction, murder, and blackmail and sentenced to life in prison. Associated Press, *Schoolboy's Killer Gets Life Sentence*, INT'L. HERALD TRIB., July 29, 2003, at http://www.iht.com/articles/104393.html.

26. AMNESTY INT'L., TORTURE WORLDWIDE: AN AFFRONT TO HUMAN DIGNITY.

27. *Id.* at 3.

28. AMNESTY INT'L., AMNESTY INTERNATIONAL REPORT 2004: TORTURE AND ILL-TREATMENT, available at http://www.amnesty.org/resources/report04/stats-eng/text/03.html. The United States, Canada, Japan, France, Italy, Spain, and Germany have all ratified the UN Convention against Torture. See RATIFICATIONS AND RESERVATIONS, OFFICE OF THE UNITED NATIONS HIGH COMMISSIONER FOR HUMAN RIGHTS, at http://www.ohchr.org/english/countries/ratification/9.htm.

29. *Conclusions and Recommendations of the Committee against Torture: Israel*, U.N. HCHR, 27th Sess., U.N. Doc. CAT/C/XXVII/Concl.5 (2001), available at http://www.unhchr.ch/tbs/doc.nsf/; *see also* John T. Parry & Welsh S. White, *Interrogating Suspected Terrorists: Should Torture Be an Option?*, 63 U. PITT. L. REV. 743, 757–60 (2002). As noted in chapter 1, the Israeli government denied that the force used in interrogations of Palestinians constituted torture.

30. Not all forms of physical interrogation were banned as illegal. In particular, methods—including sleep deprivation—are allowed if incidental to the interrogation process and the defense of necessity might be available to interrogators who use physical pressure. AMNESTY INT. USA, COMMITTEE AGAINST TORTURE SAYS ISRAEL'S POLICY OF CLOSURES AND DEMOLITIONS OF

PALESTINIAN HOMES MAY AMOUNT TO CRUEL, INHUMAN, OR DEGRADING TREATMENT (2001), at http://www.amnestyusa.org/news/2001/israel11232001.html.

31. *Concluding Observations of the Committee against Torture: Israel*, U.N. HCHR, U.N. Doc. A/52/44 (1997), available at http://www.unhchr.ch/tbs/doc.nsf/.

32. See generally Associated Foreign Press, *Israeli Forces Increasing Use of Torture*, GLOBAL EXCHANGE, Nov. 21, 2001, at http://www.globalexchange.org/countries/palestine/news/2001/afp112101.html.pf; see also Yuval Ginbar, PUBLIC COMM. AGAINST TORTURE IN ISRAEL, BACK TO A ROUTINE OF TORTURE: TORTURE AND ILL-TREATMENT OF PALESTINIAN DETAINEES DURING ARREST, DETENTION, AND INTERROGATION—SEPTEMBER 2001–APRIL 2003.

33. Pub. Comm. against Torture in Israel v. State of Israel, 38 I.L.M.1471, 1486 (1999). Parry and White have recently advocated the introduction of a "necessity" defense for torture in the United States. They argue that while torture should never be authorized, a defense of "necessity" should be available to a government agent using torture if that agent can prove his actions "were necessary to avert a greater, imminent harm." John T. Parry and Welsh S. White, *Interrogating Suspected Terrorists: Should Torture Be an Option?* 63 U. PITT. L. REV. 743 (2002) 762–63. This proposal is unsound for several reasons. First, an unshakable rule of virtue is that the law must be knowable. This means that transparent legal standards must exist in order that people can shape their conduct to comply with the law. Given the heavy price that individuals can pay if they break the law, the lawfulness of one's conduct should not be left to chance. Secondly, there is little practical difference between authorizing torture prior to the act and effectively authorizing it by providing the perpetrators with legal defense after the act. In both cases, there will be no adverse consequences for agents who torture others in circumstances where the torture is morally justifiable. The key difference is that if the criteria where torture is desirable are not spelled out at the outset, this will make it more difficult for interrogators to determine when their actions

are justifiable. Parry and White believe this to be a positive, suggesting that either ignorance of the availability of the defense or uncertainty about whether the defense would be available would promote deterrence. *Id.* It is dubious logic to enact a law that relies on ignorance or ambiguity to achieve the desired result. Moreover, it is not feasible to attempt to try to "hide" the existence of a legal defense. After it was successfully used once, its existence would become widely known. Thirdly, there is some merit in the view that making the scope of the defense might make people reluctant to engage in acts of torture. However, this begs the question as far as legislating for the limited use of torture is concerned. It assumes that it is desirable that people should be discouraged from engaging in limited acts of torture and hence prejudges the moral content of such a law. If life-saving torture is in fact desirable (as Parry and White agree), then people should not be deterred from engaging in such conduct. They should in fact be given a green light to do so, and this can be best achieved by providing a legal framework that to the maximum extent possible sets out when life-saving torture is permissible. This framework is set out in chapter 3.

34. These are referred to by the authorities as "exceptional means of interrogation." Yuval Ginbar, PUBLIC COMM. AGAINST TORTURE IN ISRAEL, BACK TO A ROUTINE OF TORTURE: TORTURE AND ILL-TREATMENT OF PALESTINIAN DETAINEES DURING ARREST, DETENTION, AND INTERROGATION—SEPTEMBER 2001–APRIL 2003, at 17.

35. *Id.* at 20.

36. *Id.* at 21.

37. *Id.* at 22.

38. U.S. DEP'T. OF STATE, TURKEY: COUNTRY REPORTS ON HUMAN RIGHTS PRACTICES—2003, 1 (Feb. 25, 2004), available at www.state.gov/g/drl/rls/hrrpt/2003/27869pf.htm; see also, AMNESTY INT'L., TURKEY: AN END TO TORTURE AND IMPUNITY IS OVERDUE! (Oct. 2001), http://www.amnestyusa.org/stoptorture/turkey_torture_report.rtf.

39. *Id.*

40 U.S. DEP'T. OF STATE, PAKISTAN: COUNTRY REPORTS ON HUMAN RIGHTS PRACTICES—2003, 5 (Feb. 25, 2004), available at www.state.gov/g/drl/rls/hrrpt/2003/27950pf.htm.

41. U.S. DEP'T. OF STATE, CHINA (INCLUDES TIBET, HONG KONG, AND MACAU): COUNTRY REPORTS ON HUMAN RIGHTS PRACTICES—2003, 7 (Feb. 25, 2004) (internal citations omitted), available at www.state.gov/g/drl/rls/hrrpt/2003/27768pf.htm; see also AMNESTY INT'L., TORTURE—A GROWING SCOURGE IN CHINA (Feb. 2001) at http://www.amnestyusa.org/interfaith/document.do?id=5DE714C0187DFD31802569DD0041B35C.

42. U.S. DEP'T. OF STATE, PHILIPPINES: COUNTRY REPORTS ON HUMAN RIGHTS PRACTICES—2003, 4 (Feb. 25, 2004), available at www.state.gov/g/drl/rls/hrrpt/2003/27786pf.htm.

43. See generally *Shock, Outrage over Prison Photos*, CNN, May 1, 2004, at http://www.cnn.com/2004/WORLD/meast/04/30/iraq.photos/. See further, Mark Danner, TORTURE AND TRUTH: AMERICA, ABU GHRAIB, AND THE WAR ON TERROR (2004); Seymour M. Hersh, CHAIN OF COMMAND: THE ROAD FROM 9/11 TO ABU GHRAIB (2004).

44. *Id.*

45. ART. 15–6, INVESTIGATION OF THE 800TH MILITARY POLICY BRIGADE 16–18 (2004), available at http://news.bbc.co.uk/nol/shared/bsp/hi/pdfs/10_5_04_tagubareport.pdf (this report of the investigation conducted by Major General Antonio Taguba is labeled "Secret/No Foreign Dissemination" but has been published on the BBC News Web site).

46. AMNESTY INT'L., IRAQ: AMNESTY INTERNATIONAL REVEALS A PATTERN OF TORTURE AND ILL-TREATMENT, May 26, 2004, at http://web.amnesty.org/web/web.nsf/prnt/irq-torture-eng; see also Susan Sontag, *Regarding the Torture of Others*, N.Y. TIMES, LATE ED., May 23, 2004, at 25; AMNESTY INT'L., AMNESTY INTERNATIONAL REPORT 2004: IRAQ, 3, at http://web.amnesty.org/web/web.nsf/print/2004–irq-summary-eng. Ken Coates, *The Creeping Sickness*, GUARDIAN (United Kingdom), Mar. 13, 2004, available at http://www.guardian.co.uk/guantanamo/story/0,13743,1168592,00.html.

47. AMNESTY INT'L., IRAQ: HUMAN RIGHTS PROTECTION AND
PROMOTION VITAL IN THE TRANSITIONAL PERIOD, at http://
www.amnestyusa.org/women/document.do?id=23055999CF85
3CD680256EB60052AE1C.

48. *Id.*

49. Elif Kaban, *The United Nations Rebukes The U.S. over
Brutality in Prisons*, REUTERS, May 15, 2000, at http://www.
prisons.org/un.htm.

50. *Id.*

51. See, e.g., *The Legal Prohibition against Torture*, HUM.
RTS. WATCH, Mar. 11, 2003, at A2, at http://www.hrw.org/press/
2001/11/TortureQandA.htm; Dana Priest and Barton Gellman,
U.S. Decries Abuse but Defends Interrogations, WASH. POST,
Dec. 26, 2002, at A01.

52. Dana Priest and Barton Gellman, *U.S. Decries Abuse
but Defends Interrogations*.

53. James Silver, *Why America's Top Liberal Lawyer Wants
to Legalise Torture*, THE SCOTSMAN, May 22, 2004, available at
http://thescotsman.scotsman.com/international.cfm?id=582662
004.

54. See, e.g., AMNESTY INT'L., EGYPT: TORTURE REMAINS
RIFE AS CRIES FOR JUSTICE GO UNHEEDED (Feb. 2001), at http://
web.amnesty.org/ai.nsf/Index/MDE120012001?OpenDocu-
ment&of=COUNTRIES\EGYPT; AMNESTY INT'L., MEXICO: JUS-
TICE BETRAYED—TORTURE IN THE JUDICIAL SYSTEM (June 2001),
at   http://www.amnestyusa.org/stoptorture/mexico_justice_
betrayed.pdf; AMNESTY INT'L., ALBANIA: TORTURE AND ILL-
TREATMENT—AN END TO IMPUNITY (May 18, 2001), at http://
web.amnesty.org/ai.nsf/print/EUR110012001?OpenDocument;
AMNESTY INT'L; Renata Capella and Michael Sfard, THE ASSASSI-
NATION POLICY OF THE STATE OF ISRAEL: NOVEMBER 2000–JANU-
ARY 2002, The Public Committee against Torture in Israel
(PCATI) and LAW—The Palestinian Society for the Protection
of Human Rights and the Environment (May 2002).

3. THE MORAL STATUS OF TORTURE

1. John Rawls, A THEORY OF JUSTICE 27–28 (1971).

2. See Tom Campbell, THE LEGAL THEORY OF ETHICAL POSITIVISM 161–88 (1996).

3. Stanley I. Benn, *Human Rights—For Whom and for What?*, in HUMAN RIGHTS 59, 61 (Eugene Kamenka and Alice Erh-Soon Tay, eds., 1978).

4. Tom Campbell, *Realizing Human Rights*, in HUMAN RIGHTS: FROM RHETORIC TO REALITY 1, 13 (Tom Campbell et al., eds., 1996).

5. Almost to the point where it is not too far off the mark to propose that the "escalation of rights rhetoric is out of control." L. Wayne Sumner, THE MORAL FOUNDATION OF RIGHTS 1 (1987).

6. *Id.*

7. H. L. A. Hart, ESSAYS IN JURISPRUDENCE AND PHILOSOPHY 196–97 (1983).

8. UDHR, G.A. Res. 217 A(III), U.N. Doc. A/810 at 71 (1948) [hereinafter UDHR] at art. 3; ICCPR G.A. Res. 2200A (XXI), U.N. GOAR, 21st Sess., Supp. No. 16, at 52, U.N. Doc. A/6316 (1966) at 51.

9. UDHR, at art. 3; ICCPR, at art. 9.

10. UDHR, 16, at art. 5; ICCPR, 17, at art. 7.

11. UDHR, at art. 22; International Covenant on Economic, Social, and Cultural Rights, G.A. Res. 2200A (XXI), Dec. 16, 1966, arts. 9 & 15 [hereinafter ICESCR].

12. UDHR, at art. 12; ICCPR, at art. 17.

13. UDHR, at art. 24; ICESCR, at art. 7(d).

14. UDHR, at art. 25; ICESCR, at art. 11.

15. Ronald Dworkin, TAKING RIGHTS SERIOUSLY (4th ed., 1978).

16. *Id.* at 193.

17. *Id.* at 193.

18. *Id.* at 194.

19. *Id.* at 198.

20. *Id.* at 199; see also, *Liberalism*, in PUBLIC AND PRIVATE MORALITY 113, 127, 136 (1979).

21. Ronald Dworkin, TAKING RIGHTS SERIOUSLY, *supra* note 15, at 272.

22. *Id.*

23. Nozick begins by imagining that no state exists. He then details the type of state that is legitimate and that he believes people would mold consistent with their moral rights. Through this process he claims that we would at the minimal state a position between anarchy and a redistributive state. In this state, fetters on freedom are few. Individuals have power to own and transfer property and to hire the labor of others. The state has an extremely minimalist role, its functions being confined to those that are essentially protective in nature. Basically, the state can only protect against such matters as force, theft, and enforcement of contracts, and so on. It cannot implement paternalist measures or coerce citizens to aid others. Thus, the state cannot assume private property or impose taxes in order to, say, redistribute resources to the disadvantaged. Roles such as this, if they are to be undertaken, must be left to private individuals and enterprises. This is the type of state, a pure form of capitalism, Nozick claims will emerge through an "invisible hand process" by rational people acting in a self-interested manner. Nozick says that this type of minimal state is the best way to ensure that rights are not violated. A more powerful state would impinge upon individual rights and is, hence, unjustifiable unless people unanimously waive some of their rights to establish such a state. Robert Nozick, ANARCHY, STATE, AND UTOPIA 206–7 (1974).

24. *Id.*

25. Nozick believes that the paramountcy accorded to the right of self-ownership and liberty is necessary to protect people from the burdensome demands of competing moral theories

such as utilitarianism. For example, he believes only his rights theory can protect people from such ghastly violations as forced organ donations where the donations would maximize happiness by saving the lives of many or assisting those most in need. NOZICK, *supra*, note 23, at 206–7.

26. Nozick goes on to develop a retributive theory of punishment from his general moral theory. Nozick advances a communicative theory of punishment in which he claims that punishment is justified on the basis that it reconnects the offender with the correct values from which his wrongdoing has disconnected him.

27. Mirko Bagaric, *In Defence of a Utilitarian Theory of Punishment: Punishing the Innocent and the Compatibility of Utilitarianism and Rights*, 24 AUSTL. J. OF LEGAL PHIL. 95, 121–43 (1999); Mirko Bagaric, SENTENCING AND PUNISHMENT: A RATIONAL APPROACH, ch. 4 (2001).

28. Tom Campbell, JUSTICE 52 (1st ed., 1990).

29. See e.g., Michael Tooley, *Abortion and Infanticide*, in APPLIED ETHICS 64–71 (P. Singer, ed., 1986); Peter Singer, *All Animals Are Equal*, in APPLIED ETHICS 215, 215–16 (P. Singer, ed., 1986).

30. See John Kleinig, *Human Rights, Legal Rights, and Social Change*, in HUMAN RIGHTS 36, 40 (Eugene Kamenka and Alice Erh-Soon Tay, eds., 1978).

31. Stanley I. Benn, *Rights*, in THE ENCYCLOPEDIA OF PHILOSOPHY vol. 7, at 196 (Paul Edwards, ed., 1967).

32. Ronald Dworkin, *supra* note 15, 201.

33. Nozick, *supra* note 23, 95.

34. H. L. A. Hart, ESSAYS IN JURISPRUDENCE AND PHILOSOPHY 195 (1983).

35. Tom Campbell, JUSTICE 52 (1st ed., 1990), at 165.

36. *Id.*

37. See, e.g., G. J. Warnock, CONTEMPORARY MORAL PHILOSOPHY 24–26 (1967).

38. See J. J. C. Smart, *An Outline of a System of Utilitarian Ethics*, in UTILITARIANISM: FOR AND AGAINST 1 (J. J. C. Smart and Bernard Williams, eds., 1973).

39. See, e.g. B. Williams, *A Critique of Utilitarianism*, in UTILITARIANISM: FOR AND AGAINST 12–16.

40. See H. J. McCloskey, META-ETHICS AND NORMATIVE ETHICS 180–82 (1969).

41. See Robert Nozick, ANARCHY, STATE, AND UTOPIA 206–7 (1974).

42. See, e.g., Jeremy Bentham, *Value of a Lot of Pleasure or Pain, How to Be Measured*, in AN INTRODUCTION TO THE PRINCIPLES OF MORALS AND LEGISLATION (1907) (first published 1789). This work has been cited by Dershowitz as providing "the most powerful utilitarian case for limited torture of convicted criminals to gather information necessary to prevent serious future crime." Alan M. Dershowitz, *The Torture Warrant: A Response to Professor Strauss*, 48 N.Y.L. SCH. L. REV. 275, 275–76 (2004).

43. H. J. McCloskey, META-ETHICS AND NORMATIVE ETHICS 180–82 (1969), at 180–81.

44. See, e.g., T. L. S. Sprigge, *A Utilitarian Reply to Dr. McCloskey,* 8 INQUIRY 264, 272 (1965).

45. As an example, McCloskey's hypothetical could be altered by providing that the town was an isolated one, hence there is no opportunity for help arriving before the riots occurred. Also, the crime should be murder, not a rape, in which case there is one less person who could reveal the miscarriage of justice that has occurred, and thus the risk of a possible loss of respect and confidence in the law is not as significant.

46. While this is not normally the case, i.e., we normally like to think that we send our soldiers into situations with at least a fighting chance, there are countless reported instances of men being ordered to go or remain in situations that can only be described as suicide missions. For those men who voluntarily place themselves in such situations, it is rather illuminating that

the proscription against suicide disappears. They are heroes rather than bad men—they followed the dictates of utilitarianism.

47. Manuel Velasquez and Cynthia Rostankowski, ETHICS: THEORY AND PRACTICE 103–6 (1985).

48. See *id.*

49. See Manuel Velasquez and Cynthia Rostankowski, ETHICS: THEORY AND PRACTICE. A famous modern day example that comes closest to the dilemma of choosing whether to frame the innocent or tolerate massive abuses of rights followed the Rodney King beating in Los Angeles on March 3, 1991. The policemen who beat King were acquitted under state law of any offense regarding the incident. Riots ensued, resulting in widespread looting, damage to property, and dozens of deaths. Shortly afterwards, the government announced the almost unprecedented step that the policemen, who were found innocent of the alleged crime, were to be tried on federal charges regarding the incident. They were duly found guilty, despite the apparent double jeopardy involved. See David Cole, NO EQUAL JUSTICE: RACE AND CLASS IN THE AMERICAN JUSTICE SYSTEM 23 (1999), for discussion of this incident. Whatever one's view of the government's motivation for charging the policemen, it seems that justice took a back seat, at least for a while.

50. This has been used as an argument against a naturalistic view of morality. However, see C. R. Pigden, *Naturalism*, in A COMPANION TO ETHICS 421, 422–26 (Peter Singer, ed., 1991), where he points out that this phenomenon simply reflects the conservative nature of logic—you cannot get out of it what you do not put in.

51. According to Mill, rights reconcile justice with utility. Justice, which he claims consists of certain fundamental rights, is merely a part of utility. "[T]o have a right is . . . to have something which society ought to defend. [If asked why] . . . I can give no other reason than general utility." John Stuart Mill, *Utilitarianism*, in UTILITARIANISM 251, 309 (Mary Warnock, ed., 1986).

52. Happiness, unlike notions such as dignity and integrity, which we have earlier criticized as being so vague as to be meaningless, is quantifiable. Recent empirical data that shows human beings are very similar in terms of the things that are conducive to well-being: Mirko Bagaric, HOW TO LIVE: BEING HAPPY AND DEALING WITH MORAL DILEMMAS (2006). In a nutshell, the things that are conducive to happiness are fit and healthy bodies, realistic goals, self-esteem, optimism, an outgoing personality, a sense of control, close relationships, challenging work, and active leisure, punctuated by adequate rest and a faith that entails communal support, purpose, and acceptance. There is only a modest connection between money and well-being. From this it is possible to establish a hierarchy of interests. The ranking (from most to least important) is life, physical integrity, food, shelter, health care, liberty, and education. Importantly, the right to life ranks above the right to physical integrity.

53. John Stuart Mill, *Utilitarianism, in* UTILITARIANISM 251, 309, at 141–83.

54. These rights, however, are never decisive and must be disregarded where they would not cause net happiness, otherwise this would be to go down the rule utilitarianism track. Rule utilitarianism is the view that the rightness of an act is assessed by reference to its compliance with rules established to maximize utility. For the rule utilitarian, the principle of utility is used as a guide for the rules we should follow, as distinct from the particular actions we should perform. Due to the difficulty in performing the utilitarian calculus necessary to determine which of a number of options we should choose, it is claimed that a set of rules guiding us in our decisions would be more likely to achieve the desired goal. The main problem with rule utilitarianism is that it is inevitable that in complying with the rules there will be occasions when happiness will not be maximized. To refuse to break the rule in such circumstances constitutes "rule-worship." See J. C. C. Smart, *An Outline of a System of Utilitarian Ethics*, in J. C. C. Smart and Bernard Williams (eds.), UTILITARIANISM: FOR AND AGAINST (1973) 3, 10. It is no answer that in most cases it is beneficial to comply with the rule;

otherwise we are putting the rule above its justification. If we do break the rule, we are still being guided by the ultimate principle: act utilitarianism; and rule utilitarianism has nothing distinctive to offer. It is not that the act utilitarian does not see general rules as playing an important role in our moral decisions, but he or she will only act in accordance with the rules where it is felt that on each particular occasion this will generate the most happiness.

55. See Joseph Raz, THE MORALITY OF FREEDOM 191 (1986). Raz also provides that such rights are useful because they enable us to settle on shared intermediary conclusions, despite considerable dispute regarding the grounds for the conclusions. *Id.*

56. See also Manfred Nowak, U.N. COVENANT ON CIVIL AND POLITICAL RIGHTS: CCPR COMMENTARY 104 (N. P. Engel 1993); Sarah Joseph, *The Right to Life*, in THE INTERNATIONAL COVENANT ON CIVIL AND POLITICAL RIGHTS AND UNITED KINGDOM LAW 155 (David Harris and Sarah Joseph, eds., 1995).

57. See Peter Singer, PRACTICAL ETHICS 85 (2nd ed., 1993).

58. The House of Lords, REPORT OF THE SELECT COMMITTEE ON MEDICAL ETHICS, vol. 1, at 13 (1994).

59. EUROPEAN CONVENTION FOR THE PROTECTION OF HUMAN RIGHTS AND FUNDAMENTAL FREEDOMS, 213 U.N.T.S. 22, Sept. 3, 1953, art. 2.

60. Dan Vergano, *Telling the Truth about Lie Detectors*, USA TODAY, 2004, available at http://www.usatoday.com/news/nation/2002–09–09–lie_x.htm (last accessed April 4, 2005).

61. ROYAL COMMISSION ON CRIMINAL JUSTICE, REPORT, UNITED KINGDOM, 1993; see also Roger Hood, RACE AND SENTENCING 125 (1992); see also P. Darbyshire, *The Mischief of Plea Bargaining and Sentencing Rewards*, CRIM. L. REV. 895, 903 (2000); M. Zander, *What on Earth Is Lord Justice Auld Supposed to Do?* CRIM. L. REV. 419 (2000).

62. *Police Threat Fuels Debate on Torture*, DEUTSCHE WELLE (Germany), Feb. 24, 2003, available at http://www.dw-world.de/english/0,3367,1430_A_785751,00.html.

63. Interview by Wolf Blitzer with Alan Dershowitz, Professor of Law, Harvard University, and Ken Roth, *Dershowitz: Torture Could Be Justified* (Mar. 3, 2003), available at http://edition.cnn.com/2003/LAW/03/03/cnna.Dershowitz. Dershowitz came across the idea for "torture warrants" while reading about sixteenth- and seventeenth-century England and France. While the French were torturing "virtually everybody," the English Privy Council insisted on warrants. This led to about 100 people being tortured over the course of a century. See James Silver (quoting Alan Dershowitz), *Why America's Top Liberal Lawyer Wants to Legalise Torture*, THE SCOTSMAN, May 22, 2004, available at: http://thescotsman.scotsman.com/international.cfm?id=582662004.

64. Id.

4. THE SLIPPERY SLOPE ILLUSION

1. For example, Anne O'Rourke et al., *Torture, Slippery Slope, Intellectual Apologists, and Ticking Bombs: An Australian Response to Bagaric and Clarke* 40 U.S.F. L. REV. (2006); Philip N. S. Rumney, *Is Coercive Interrogation of Terrorist Suspects Effective?* 40 U.S.F. L. REV. (2006).

2. *Id.* (quoting Ken Roth, the executive director of Human Rights Watch). It has been suggested that Israel ended up torturing around 90 percent of the Palestinian security detainees they had until finally the Israeli supreme court outlawed the practice. *Id.*; see also John T. Parry and Welsh S. White, *Interrogating Suspected Terrorists: Should Torture Be an Option?* 63 U. PITT. L. REV. 743 (2002) 764.

3. For a discussion of the use and persuasiveness of the argument, see Kumar Amarasekara and Mirko Bagaric, MORALITY AND THE LAW, ch. 4 (2002).

4. The most recent annual United Nations Food and Agriculture Organization report notes that present levels of hunger

cause the deaths of more than six million children a year. In terms of more comprehensible figures, this equates to more than 16,000 daily deaths from hunger; see Food and Agriculural Organization of the United Nations, STATE OF FOOD INSECURITY IN THE WORLD 2005.

5. F. M. Cornford, *The Microcosmographia Academica* (1908) 23.

6. Alan M. Dershowitz, *The Torture Warrant: A Response to Professor Strauss*, 48 N.Y.L. SCH. L. REV. 275, 283 (2003).

7. Dershowitz, for example, has stated, "People say 'Oh my God, that will open the floodgates.' I say the reverse is true. I believe that would close the floodgates. My view is that accountability . . . will reduce the amount of torture rather than increase it." James Silver (quoting Alan Dershowitz), *Why America's Top Liberal Lawyer Wants to Legalise Torture*, THE SCOTSMAN, May 22, 2004, available at http://thescotsman.scotsman.com/international.cfm?id=582662004.

8. Deborah Hope, *The End Justifies the Pain*, THE AUSTRALIAN, December 10, 2005; Maria Moscaritolo, *The Gloves Are Off*, ADELAIDE ADVERTISER, Dec. 9, 2005.

9. While some theorists believe that this has a retributive rationale, in our view the key justification for sentencing is utilitarianism; see Mirko Bagaric, PUNISHMENT AND SENTENCING: A RATIONAL APPROACH (2001).

10. Conclusions drawn regarding euthanasia cannot be applied to the torture setting, since euthanasia does not involve setting off one person's interests against other.

11. The Israel experience comes closest to our proposal, but there are enormous differences. The criteria for torture were extremely broad: "So long as the interrogator reasonably believes the lesser evil of force is necessary to get information, that would prevent the greater evil of loss of innocent lives." John T. Parry and Welsh S. White, *Interrogating Suspected*

Terrorists: Should Torture Be an Option? 63 U. PITT. L. REV. 743, 757–60 (2002). Note that there is no requirement that torture be used as a last resort and that it is almost certain that the suspect has the relevant knowledge. The torture guidelines were not law but internal police guidelines, and there was no meaningful overview of practices: *ibid.* It could only be in such a climate that most (85 percent) Palestinian detainees were reported to have been tortured: B'Tselem, ROUTINE TORTURE: INTERROGATION METHODS OF THE GENERAL SECURITY SERVICE 30 (1998), 5.

5. LIFE-SAVING TORTURE IS A HUMANE PRACTICE

1. This is a point made by several critics. See, for example, John Kleinig, *Ticking Bombs and Torture Warrants* 10 DEAKIN L. REV. 614, 620 (2005).

2. Obviously, there are points of dissimilarity between surgery and torture. An obvious point of departure is that surgery is intended to benefit the person upon whom the pain is inflicted. However, this analogy is not advanced as a knockdown argument in favor of torture. Rather, it is advanced merely to refute the claim that deliberately inflicting pain on another person necessarily damages the agent that inflicts the pain.

3. See, for example, Anne O'Rourke et al., *Torture, Slippery Slope, Intellectual Apologists, and Ticking Bombs: An Australian Response to Bagaric and Clarke* 40 U.S.F. L. REV. 11–12 (2005).

4. See M. Bagaric, *A Utilitarian Argument: Laying the Foundation for a Coherent System of Law* 10 OTAGO L. REV. (NZ) 163 (2002), where it is argued that morality is an objective inquiry.

5. See further, Alasdair Palmer, in *Is Torture Always Wrong?* THE SPECTATOR 40–42, September 24, 2005, who notes that the ban on torture is inconsistent with the acceptance of a shoot-to-kill policy in some circumstances.

6. TORTURE IS EFFECTIVE

1. Philip N. S. Rumney, *Is Coercive Interrogation of Terrorist Suspects Effective?* 40 U.S.F L. REV. (2006).

2. Even O'Rourke et al., concede this; see Anne O'Rourke et al., *Torture, Slippery Slope, Intellectual Apologists, and Ticking Bombs: An Australian Response to Bagaric and Clarke.*

3. Marcy Strauss, *Torture* 48 N.Y.L. SCH. L. REV. 201, 264 (2003–2004).

4. Eric A. Posner and Adrian Vermeule, *Should Coercive Interrogation Be Legal?* (U. OF CHI. PUB. L. AND LEGAL THEORY WORKING PAPER No. 84, 2, 2005).

5. Adam Shatz, *The Torture of Algiers*, N.Y. REV. BOOKS Nov. 21, 2002, 53, 57.

6. As cited in Alasdair Palmer, *Is Torture Always Wrong?* THE SPECTATOR, 40–41, September 24, 2005. The book is THE BATTLE OF CASBAH: TERRORISM AND COUNTERTERRORISM IN ALGERIA, 1955–57.

7. Evan Thomas and Michelle Hirsch, *The Debate over Torture*, NEWSWEEK, November 21, 2005, http://www.msnbc.msn.com/id/10020629/site/newsweek.

8. THE INTERROGATORS: INSIDE THE SECRET WAR AGAINST AL-QA'EDA, as cited in Alasdair Palmer, in *Is Torture Always Wrong?* THE SPECTATOR, 41, September 24, 2005.

9. Alasdair Palmer, *Is Torture Always Wrong?* THE SPECTATOR, 40, September 24, 2005. He goes on to give numerous other examples of where torture has been effective obtaining information and thwart attacks on innocent people.

10. Marcy Strauss, *Torture* 48 N.Y.L. SCH. L. REV. 201 (2004).

11. D. Espo and L. Sidoti, *Cheney Bid for Torture Ban Exemption*, THE AGE, 9, Nov. 6, 2005.

12. David Sanger, *Bush Confident of Deal in Tough Question*, THE AGE, Dec. 14, 2005, 17.

13. Francis Harris, *Bush Forced to Accept Torture Ban*, THE AGE, Dec. 17, 2005, 15.

14. *Torture Ban Has Exceptions*, HERALD SUN, Dec. 20, 2005, http://www.heraldsun.news.com.au/common/story_page/0,5478,17609059%255E1702,00.html.

15. Ibid.

16. Deborah Hope, *The End Justifies the Pain*, THE AUSTRALIAN, Dec. 10, 2005.

17. See Alan Dershowitz, *Warming Up on Torture*, LA TIMES, Oct. 17, 2006.

18. Philip N. S. Rumney, *Is Coercive Interrogation of Terrorist Suspects Effective?* 40 U.S.F. L. REV. (2006).

19. A similar point is made by Marcy Strauss, *Torture* 48 N.Y.L. SCH. L. REV. 201 (2004).

20. See examples given by Marcy Strauss, in *Torture* 48 N.Y.L. SCH. L. REV. 201 (2004). See further, Charles Whitbread and Christopher Slobogin, CRIMINAL PROCEDURE: AN ANALYSIS OF CASES AND CONCEPTS 401 (4th ed., 2000).

7. TORTURE IS NOT ANTIDEMOCRATIC

1. Anne O'Rourke et al., *Torture, Slippery Slope, Intellectual Apologists, and Ticking Bombs: An Australian Response to Bagaric and Clarke* 40 U.S.F. L. REV. (2005).

2. Evan Thomas and Michelle Hirsch, *The Debate over Torture*, NEWSWEEK, Nov. 21, 2005: http://www.msnbc.msn.com/id/10020629/site/newsweek.

3. *Poll Finds Broad Approval of Terrorist Torture—Americas*, MSNBC.com, http://www.msnbc.msn.com/id/10345320/print/1/displaymode/1098.

4. For a discussion of this case, see Mirko Bagaric, *The Jodie and Marie Siamese Twins Case—The Problem with Rights* 8 J. OF L. & MED. 311–21 (2001).

5. *Re A (Children)* [2000] 4 All ER 961, 1006.

6. See report of the case by S. Moynihan, *Underworld Lawyer Found Guilty of Contempt*, THE AGE, 3, Nov. 15, 2005.

7. Samuel Freeman, *Original Meaning, Democratic Interpretation, and the Constitution* 21 PHILOSOPHY AND PUBLIC AFFAIRS 3, 22 (1992).

8. Alasdair Palmer, in *Is Torture Always Wrong?* THE SPECTATOR, Sept. 24, 2005, 42.

8. THE REAL DIVIDE: WHERE RESPONSIBILITY STARTS AND ENDS

1. As cited in Philip N. S. Rumney, *Is Coercive Interrogation of Terrorist Suspects Effective?* 40 U.S.F. L. REV. (2006).

2. Bernard Williams, A CRITIQUE OF UTILITARIANISM, in J. C. C. Smart and Bernard Williams (eds.), *Utilitarianism: For and Against* (1973) 99.

3. Ibid. 112.

4. See Mirko Bagaric and Penny Dimpolous, *Human Rights: All Show, No Go* 4 J. OF HUMAN RIGHTS 3 (2005).

9. WHY THE TORTURE DEBATE *REALLY* MATTERS

1. M. Bagaric and J. McConvill, *Goodbye Justice, Hello Happiness: Human Well-being as the New Benchmark for the Development of the Law—Welcoming Positive Psychology to the Law* 10 DEAKIN L. REV. 1 (2005).

2. See further, Mirko Bagaric and Penny Dimpolous, *Human Rights: All Show, No Go.*

3. Pamela Bone, *"We Can Be What We Eat"* THE AGE, 12, Mar. 12, 2005.

4. See Mirko Bagaric and Sharon Erbacher, *Fat and the Law: Who Should Take the Blame?* 12 J. OF L. AND MED. 323 (2005).

5. This is not to suggest that all the critics of our proposal have fallen into the trap of allowing emotion to win the day. As noted above, the article by Rumney is excellent. Although not a response to our proposal, other measured and clear-thinking pieces that take a contrary approach to my proposal include: John T. Parry and Welsh S. White, *Interrogating Suspected Terrorists: Should Torture Be an Option?* 63 U. PITT. L. REV. 743, 764 (2002) and Marcy Strauss, *Torture* 48 N.Y.L. SCH. L. REV. 201 (2004).

6. Kate Gibbs, *Profession Attacks Torture Vision*, LAWYER'S WEEKLY, 1 May 27, 2005.

7. Liz Minchin, *Deakin Staff, Students Rally on Torture Backing*, THE AGE, May 27, 2005.

8. Peter Singer, *All Animals are Equal*, in P. Singer (ed.), APPLIED ETHICS 215, 228 (1986).

9. Desmond Munderson, *Another Modest Proposal*, 10 DEAKIN L. REV. 641, 651 (2005).

10. See John T. Parry and Welsh S. White, *Interrogating Suspected Terrorists: Should Torture Be an Option?* 63 U. PITT. L. REV. 743, 764 (2002).

11. For an argument that necessity does not permit torture, see P. Gaeta, (2004) 2 J.I.C.L. 785, but see John T. Parry and Welsh S. White, *Interrogating Suspected Terrorists: Should Torture Be an Option?* 63 U. PITT. L. REV. 743, 764 (2002).

12. The new provisions states:

(1) A person is not guilty of a relevant offense in respect of conduct carried out by him or her in response to circumstances of sudden or extraordinary emergency.

(2) This section applies if and only if the person carrying out the conduct reasonably believes that—
  (a) circumstances of sudden or extraordinary emergency exist; and
  (b) committing the offense is the only reasonable way to deal with the emergency; and
  (c) the conduct is a reasonable response to the emergency.

(3) This section only applies in the case of murder if the emergency involves a risk of death or really serious injury.

13. Eric A. Posner and Adrian Vermeule, *Should Coercive Interrogation Be Legal?* U. CHI. PUB. L. AND LEGAL THEORY WORKING PAPER No. 84, 2 (2005), believe that there are other reasons for the taboo in relation to torture. They speculate that it might be in part due to "concern for reputation, social influences, and fear of ostracism" along with the common "herding" process where people blindly follow the "lead" of others.

Index